THE
ANCESTORS

*An enthralling true tale spanning three generations of
one family who lived in the Caribbean in years gone by.*

Jean Bovell

JEAN BOVELL

Published by BookPublishing World 2013

ISBN: 978-1-909204-31-7

BookPublishingWorld
An imprint of Dolman SCott

www.dolmanscott.com

This book is dedicated to
Rosie Radix-Williams & Eileen Radix-Mackintosh

INTRODUCTION

The Ancestors is based on a true story. It tracks the lineage of three first daughters who hailed from a small rural community on a Caribbean island between 1845 and 1883.

These were women of substance with strong characters, courage, self-belief and determination. They lived during a period in their community when women were generally disadvantaged and resigned to lives of toil, subservience and child-bearing.

The narrative gives an account of the women's lives, loves and marriages and how they overcame obstacles and succeeded in fulfilling personal aspirations and goals. It lingers on the highs and lows of the granddaughter's fortuitous marriage and includes separate synopses into the characteristics of her remarkable offspring.

Significant national and international events that occurred during our heroines' journey are incorporated and characters are illuminated as the reader is taken back in time to a place where people lived simple and unhurried lives.

The Ancestors is a readable, compelling and uplifting biopic which details the setbacks and triumphs across three generations of a family on their climb from the bottom of the valley to the top of the hill during an age when higher educational opportunities were largely inaccessible to people from humble Caribbean communities.

CONTENTS

THE ANCESTORS

THE BEGINNING

The discovery of the Americas by the Italian explorer Christopher Columbus and his fleet of ships in 1492 was destined to be momentously impactful on world history. Columbus united the Eastern and Western Hemispheres. He opened a route across the Atlantic to the new world and was widely known as The Discoverer during the 19th century.

One particular island, with uninhabited islets dotted not far from its shores, was among many beautiful islands uncovered by Columbus and his crew during their magnificent voyage of discovery.

The navigators were captivated by the uniqueness of the island's picturesque landscapes, copious greenery, scenic mountains, lush hills and valleys and plantations of different varieties of tropical fruit, vegetables, ground provision, herbs, peppers and spices, and nuts such as cashews and almonds.

Many miles of untouched silver sands fringed with statuesque coconut-laden trees bordered the western coastline. There were splendid views of the Atlantic along the eastern coast.

On discovery, the island was found to be inhabited by a friendly and gentle tribe of Indians known as Arawaks. They lived in groups on settlements of huts that were made from sticks and leaves and covered with large palms.

Columbus named this unique and serene land Conception Island. Conception Island was some time later invaded by a tribe of Amerindians from South America better known as Caribs. The gentle and defenceless Arawaks were conquered and killed by the warrior-like Caribs and they renamed the newly invaded island Camerhogue. After many years, Spanish sailors voyaging along the Caribbean Sea were struck by Camerhogue's landscapes and their similarity to those in Spain, and decided to christen the island Granada.

COLONISATION

Granada was initially colonised by France and, when the first French settlers arrived in 1650, the Caribs took up arms in defence of their land. They fought bravely and fiercely, but were unable to match the power and sophistication of French armoury and lost every battle. Caribs were a proud and courageous people, and those who survived the bloody massacre chose to jump to their deaths at Le Morne de Sauteurs, rather than surrender to the Colonialists.

Granada became known as La Grenade under French rule and by the year 1761 was divided into six parishes. Each parish contained a town centre in which there were retail outlets, a post office, police station and Catholic Church. Roads had been laid in every parish and several led to beaches. Estates had been established and maps of the island were in existence.

Slaves were shipped into La Grenade from West Africa and made to work the land for extended periods in blazing sun or thunderous rain. The majority were nonetheless treated with a degree of consideration by French planters, mindful that their labouring tasks were crucially contributory to the economy of the island. La Grenade slaves were permitted to help themselves to produce that was needed for their separate purposes and were also paid a small wage. People from slave communities were indoctrinated into Christianity, baptised into the Faith and encouraged to live Christian lives. In particular, promiscuity was discouraged and marriage promoted.

La Grenade was surrendered to the British under the Treaty of Paris in 1763 and from that point onwards La Grenade was called Grenada. The island would also in the future be known as the Isle of Spice or Spice Island.

During French rule, the original names of slaves were replaced with those carried by French planters. Following British takeover, the majority of slaves found that the names to which they had grown accustomed had been once again changed and reflected those of their new British owners. Even so, the French/African sub-culture already developed in slave communities could not be easily shifted. People throughout the island who belonged to these communities held fast to their indoctrinated Roman Catholic faith, and continued to attend Church services on Sunday. But there were those who in parallel maintained old superstitious beliefs or participated in voodoo rituals. Female slaves dressed in ankle-length gathered skirts over layered petticoats, similar to those worn by French ladies of the day, but their outfits were enhanced with cultural accessories such as colourful scarves and turbans.

Grenadian slaves were required to adapt to the language of the new British Colonists. The transition from French patois to English had not been an easy process, but slaves were not only resilient but also acutely aware of their powerless status. And an original dialect of broken English spoken in distinctive tones was in time developed. But French patois was not entirely abandoned and became the second language regularly spoken among enslaved adults.

All slaves looked forward to celebratory days when feasts were followed by square dancing. The square dance was introduced by the French, but their unique version of the dance was hyped with beating drums and driven by spontaneous rhythmic excitement.

The island was recaptured by the French in 1779, but returned to British rule under the Treaty of Versailles just four years later in 1783.

Like the French, British planters were also relatively considerate in their treatment of the island's slaves and endeavoured to safeguard their welfare by appointing guardians to protect them from abuse by unscrupulous owners. Thomas Coke, a British missionary and historian, reported in 1793 that slaves in Grenada were treated with less severity than those of any other island in the region and noted the incident of a woman being fined $500 for cruelty towards her slave. The buying and selling of slaves were no less a flourishing business. An individual slave with detailed description of his or her particular physical build, skills and attributes was often included among items advertised for sale such as furniture and various bric-a-brac pieces.

People of French origin who continued to reside in Grenada following British colonisation, experienced immense loss of liberty and were even persecuted. Julien Fedon, a young revolutionary of French and African descent, had a vision to be leader of a French-speaking Roman Catholic island society in which everyone was free.

On 3rd March 1795, approximately 100 men of mixed race and African heritage headed by Fedon marched to Grenville in the middle of the night. The men broke into houses occupied by British planters and their families and at gun point ordered the planters from their beds and onto the streets, where they were shot. The village of Gouyave in the parish of St John was at the same time overtaken by a separate group of revolutionaries led by Etienne Ventour and Joachim Philip. No fatalities were incurred.

In the ensuing period slaves throughout the island were incited by Fedon and his followers to rise up against the British.

Grenada remained in the grip of Fedon and his men for 14 months. The revolutionaries were eventually defeated by the British during a battle for the capture of the capital, St George's, in May 1796. Fedon escaped by boat to the sister island of Carriacou. He was never apprehended.

ST DAVID'S

The parish of David is situated at the south-eastern end of Grenada. It sits within an area of 18 square miles and is the third largest parish after St Andrew's and St George's.

St David's is mainly an agricultural parish. Its rich red soil yields abundant traditional crops, a variety of herbs, and the aroma of spices such as nutmeg, cinnamon and cloves hang permanently in the air. There are numerous inlets, hidden beaches and small bays. French settlers named the parish Quartier du Megrin. A small coastal town called Bourg du Megrin was established by the French in 1735 and it became a busy and bustling port for the shipment of cocoa and nutmeg.

It was recorded in the slave register for St David's dated 1817 that 109 male slaves and 123 female slaves were being held in the Parish. Of the documented number of slaves, 111 had been African-born and there was in total 58 children.

On 28th August 1833, the Imperial Emancipation Act was passed requiring all slaves in British Colonies to be freed from 1st August 1834. All slaves in Grenada were freed on 1st August 1838. They received monetary remuneration, were granted rights to purchase or rent small plots of land and encouraged to pursue individual ambitions and aspirations.

Freedom was embraced with euphoria by individuals in slave communities up and down the island. They celebrated with frenetic delirium. There was much eating, drinking, jumping, shouting, beating of drums and dancing in the streets. "Free at last – Praise the Lord!" they chanted repeatedly.

But freedom came with responsibility. And after the jubilation had subsided, freed men were weighing up the benefits and disadvantages of the available choices for embarking on their newly acquired independent lives.

For many the idea of owning and cultivating plots of land, not only for subsistence but also profit, seemed an exciting prospect. Others decided to seek opportunities on the larger and more progressive island of Trinidad, where it was rumoured there was plenty of work. Those who chose to travel became the pioneers of large-scale immigration to Trinidad by Grenadians in search of comparative prosperity.

As time evolved, various sleepy villages and settlements consisting mainly of tight-knitted groups of relatives and friends emerged on rented or purchased property in St David's.

These communities were self-reliant. Individuals often assisted each other with erecting simple homes made from wood and covered with galvanise, one-room shacks constructed with mud and branches called 'straw houses', or transferring houses from one plot of land to the next. These tasks were undertaken willingly and with enthusiasm. When workers were not singing jovially in chorus, they would relay embellished tales or crack jokes in spirited tones. The working day always ended on a satisfying note with an abundance of food and drink provided by the grateful recipient. It was a period when dwellings were occupied mainly at night time and contained just one bed intended only for adults. Children were required to sleep on the floor. Lamps fuelled by kerosene were lit at dusk and switched off when everyone was ready for bed. Daily activities, including cooking, eating and socialising with friends, occurred out of doors in surrounding grounds best known as 'the yard', where animals also mingled.

Latrines were large dug-out holes surrounded by crudely erected planks of wood; but there were those who simply used the woods for that purpose. Water was sourced from natural springs, clear water streams or rivers that were sectioned for drinking and domestic use, laundering and bathing.

New communities were built on the bedrock of faith in God, hard work, a strong sense of belonging and everyone looking out for each other. Women cooked in large quantities and regularly presented each other with samples of their separate cuisine. And it was customary that visitors were provided with a generous helping of the meal of the day and would be expected to consume every morsel, whether they liked it or not. Agriculture was the main source of income and subsistence and everyone, including children, engaged in the daily grind necessary for ensuring not only the welfare of individual family units but the community as a whole. Work routines were based on an early to bed and rise schedule, the common saying being: Early to bed and early to rise makes a man healthy, wealthy and wise.

BORN FREE

In the year 1845, a 17-year-old girl called Millie, who lived on a settlement in the village of Vincennes, St David's, gave birth to her first child. It had been a long and painful labour before an infant girl was safely delivered by Millie's 36-year-old mother, Florence.

The infant's father, Tom, was 18 years of age and had been married to Millie for only a few short weeks. Florence had been ordered by her husband, Elias, to arrange the nuptials. Elias was strongly of the opinion that Tom should accept the consequences of having his way with Millie. Even so, babies being born out of wedlock were not uncommon; but Elias had married the mother of his children and was determined that other men also did right by his own daughters. It was an era in the community when adults were expected to back each other on issues or decisions concerning their respective offspring. But specific dictates from the male head of any family in their chauvinistic society were never questioned and always complied with. Tom's mother Veronica, who had assumed the position of matriarch within her single-parent household, following the demise of her own mother, felt obliged to be supportive of Elias' command. Tom had no right of opinion. Elders were at that time respected, obeyed and never challenged. Tom simply did as he was told.

The baby daughter of Millie and Tom was welcomed with great joy by everyone on the settlement. Florence was particularly happy and proud to be grandmother to such a beautiful baby, who was the first in the family to be born following emancipation.

Florence decided her grand-daughter should be called Hope. The infant was one of a new generation that had been born into freedom and it was Florence's view that the name Hope represented freedom, liberty and opportunity.

Hope's christening was planned with enthusiasm by the family and eagerly anticipated by everyone in the small community. It was an environment in which people not only relied on each other, but also knew each other's business and were welcomed at any function.

Six weeks after her birth, Hope, wrapped in white cloth, was carried to the Church in central St David's, where she was baptised in the presence of her parents, godparents and various friends and relatives.

After the church ceremony, everyone embarked on the rugged journey back to the settlement and gathered in the yard surrounding the family's simple two-roomed home.

It was a bright and sunny day, but the atmosphere in the yard was cool and calm. Heavily laden fruit trees swayed in a gentle breeze fragranced with spices. People sat on crudely made benches, large stones or trunks of nearby trees. They tucked into a meal of stewed pork and ground provision served in calabash bowls and drank ginger beer from large pan-cups. Tiny God birds flew above the heads of guests or hopped around their feet whilst competing with scrawny dogs and scurrying chickens for any morsel of food dropped.

When the eating and drinking was over, high-spirited guests chatted excitedly and simultaneously in loud voices. Tales were told, jokes were cracked and laughter was bolstered by forceful slaps and shoves. Deliriously happy youngsters jumped around gleefully or played their favourite games. It had been one of the rare days, apart from Sunday, when they were not being subjected to harsh directions and were allowed a little fun. While the jollifications were in full flow, Millie sat quietly and unnoticed on the grass with legs outstretched, patiently and contentedly breast-feeding baby Hope.

Soon there was the inevitable beating of drums and young and old were on their feet in readiness for the Square Dance. They formed into lines and joyfully clapped, jumped, skipped and changed partners in rhythm with the beat.

As dusk began to fall, guests dispersed in different directions. But spirits remained high and a glowing residual sense of pleasure was shared by all.

LIFE EVOLVES

Over the years communities of freed slaves up and down the island became increasingly organised and self-sufficient. And local skilled craftsmen such as blacksmiths, carpenters, shoemakers and tailors emerged. There were those who focused on using saved income to purchase property. Ownership of large areas of land, in those days, indicated success and commanded respect. But for everyone agriculture remained the primary source of income. In particular, the sale of nutmeg in Government-run centres provided reliable earnings. Various other products yielded from the crop such as cocoa, spices, molasses, cashew nuts and corn on the cob were sold at markets in Grenville and St George's.

Meanwhile, little Hope, who lived with her parents and younger siblings in their humble two-roomed wooden shack, had grown into a plump child with stocky legs and her cherub face was crowned with clusters of short plaits that fell haphazardly on her head.

Like many others in country communities throughout the land, the family spent daylight hours carrying out routine outdoor tasks such as looking after farm animals and working the land.

Manufactured goods were not widely available or may have been too expensive for the majority on limited incomes, and specific products were hand-prepared from source for every-day consumption.

Coffee beans and cocoa pods were picked and processed for making hot beverages. Oil was extracted from coconuts and used not only for cooking purposes but also for skin and hair care. Sugar was produced from cane. Herbs and spices, such as cinnamon, cloves, turmeric, lemon grass and ginger, were used for medicinal purposes, brewing teas, making refreshing drinks or flavourings. Hot spicy sauces were made from colourful peppers. Honey was obtained from bee hives. Farm animals were reared for milk and eggs and slaughtered for meat.

As a young and upcoming married couple with an ever-increasing family to feed, times were hard for Millie and Tom. Apart from the sewing and reaping seasons, when Millie was required to work the land alongside her husband, it was largely the case that Tom tended the crop while Millie held responsibility for the day-to-day running of the home and family, including the discipline of the children. She would allocate tasks to them such as fetching water from the river, collecting wood for building fires on which meals were cooked, running errands, feeding the animals or sweeping the yard. If they misbehaved in any way or failed to complete tasks satisfactorily, Millie would order the offender to fetch a large twig from a nearby tree and kneel on rough ground prior to being vigorously and energetically whipped. Any whimpering sounds resulted in additional blows.

Many children of the age received very little nurturing. And pent-up anger and frustration associated with being mistreated by an overbearing and unreasonable spouse was often unburdened onto the unsuspecting offspring by an exasperated mother. But children were fundamentally loved and Millie was one of a majority who demonstrated maternal affection by making sure that her siblings received large portions of food. The composition of main meals was varied, but could be some form of soup such as pea or pumpkin with dumplings. Root provision served with a little fresh or smoked meat or fish. But breadfruit, green leafy vegetables and salted meat steamed in coconut oil and commonly known as 'oil down' was always a favourite dish.

It was generally accepted that the role of a wife involved being at all times obedient, subservient and mindful of the marriage vows. Millie was totally 'under the thumb' of Tom. She was required to work the land, provide him with hearty meals, submit without reservation to his conjugal demands and look after the perennial arrival of babies. Like most wives of the day, Millie had no voice and was not respected. She was conditioned to put up, shut up and know her place. Tom could never be challenged and Millie was resigned to an existence of hardship and endurance, totally unreflective of the beautiful, bountiful and serene natural environment in which she lived.

Hope, a shrewd and intelligent child, harboured the desire to learn. It was at a time when education was not considered a priority and children were required to work like everyone else for the greater good of family and community. Like many others in communities up and down Grenada, Hope looked forward to Sunday. Dressed in her best but simple outfit, she would join with others for the four-mile barefooted walk to Church. In those days, shoes or boots were expensive commodities and were owned by very few. During the Service, Hope always offered a special prayer that her secret wish to attend the one-room school house which stood beside the Church would one day come true.

By the end of the Service most people were famished, particularly those who had been fasting from the previous night prior to receiving Holy Communion. And, enticed by thoughts of an already prepared and waiting Sunday breakfast, which may include eggs or fish cakes with fried breadfruit, washed down with coffee or 'coco tea', everyone hurriedly found their way back home.

Sunday was the only day of the week when the three main meals contained some form of meat, fish or poultry. The highly appreciated piece of meat on the bone, or even a solitary meagre 'fowl foot' at the side of a plate heaped with a variety of ground provision and vegetables, would be saved for last and leisurely chewed, sucked and enjoyed until the very last ounce of substance was fully extracted. Candies made from coconuts and sweet potato puddings were among treats provided on Sunday.

Children received no chores on the day of rest and after lunch were permitted to play or engage in hobbies such as ball games or marbles. Boys in particular were able to exercise their adventurous spirit by exploring the island. Activities included mountain climbing, hunting for wild game, catching crawfish from rivers or diving into the sea to capture tropical or shell fish. Any prized catch would be immediately placed in the large 'pan' they carried with them and cooked on a log fire before being consumed with relish.

Hope looked forward to visiting Grandma Florence during her Sunday afternoon free period and when Elias and the rest of the family were involved in their separate pursuits. Hope enjoyed spending time alone with her beloved grandmother. She would sit at Florence's feet and listen intently while grandma told stories of her experiences of slavery and how emancipation was welcomed with spontaneous jubilant celebrations all over the island. Hope loved to hear how her arrival symbolised the start of a new generation born into freedom and liberty and the joyous Christening gathering that was held to celebrate her birth. Florence would say, "Hope, I want you to have a good life. You must go and find work in Trinidad. Yuh is a pretty brown skin girl and yuh gonna be lucky der." Grandma's words stimulated an inherent sense of worth. Hope was convinced that she was no ordinary girl.

Florence confided to her grand-daughter that she secretly regretted not going to Trinidad following emancipation, but that women were not permitted to express opinions in those days. And Florence could do nothing but comply with her husband's decision to accept the option of remaining in Grenada with the prospect of purchasing plots of land.

One Sunday afternoon, while visiting with Grandma Florence, Hope revealed her secret wish to go to school, as the pair sat together under a large tree in the yard. Grandma was delighted and proud to hear that her grand-daughter desired an education and promised to do everything possible to make her dream a reality. Florence also pledged to provide Hope with a special school frock and slate and chalk, if it was 'God's will' that she should attend school.

After Hope had left for home, Grandma Florence reflected on her grand-daughter's expressed desire to attend school. It was at a time when the majority in their community were uneducated or had no concept of the value of education. And Hope's desire was the proof that assured Florence that her first grand-daughter, who had 'good colour', was indeed destined for great things.

The hierarchy in Florence's country of origin was headed by a Chief or King. These men of high status were largely responsible for selling substantial numbers of slaves to European merchants.

Purchased or captured slaves who survived the long and torturous chained journey to the new world were sold on to white plantation owners in America and the Caribbean, and were used for labouring purposes.

It became apparent that the light-skinned offspring of female slaves, impregnated by slave owners, received greater favours than their darker contemporaries. And so it was engraved into the psyche of people in slave communities that having a light complexion was the passport to a relatively increased opportunistic life.

It was indeed a courageous step taken by Florence when she hesitantly told her husband that Hope was longing to attend school. She had thoughtfully chosen the moment after soothing him into a pleasing frame of mind by serving up his favourite meal, followed by a large 'shot of rum'. Elias adored his beautiful grand-daughter, even though he considered it unmanly to show it. He feared being considered weak or soft. Florence held her breath and prayed silently as she waited for a response. However, she exhaled with relief when, after a few minutes of thought, Elias, who had no knowledge of the benefits of education, announced in a matter-of-fact fashion that if 'the girl' desired to go to school, he would ensure that her wish was granted. Before too long, Tom was carrying out his father-in-law's instructions by making sure that Hope attended school on a daily basis. But Tom did not approve of his eldest daughter having an education. In his view, Hope was 'only' a girl, who should be carrying out housekeeping chores and looking after her younger brothers and sisters, rather than waste time sitting in the school house. Tom was unable to fathom why anyone, and females in particular, should be taught how to read and write. In his view, women were put on this earth by God for the purpose of pleasing men and producing children. Furthermore, no other person in their particular community had ever been to school. But what could he do? Elias ruled the roost and everyone bowed to his demands. But Tom was determined to retain a degree of control and respect in his household by insisting that Hope carried out all her allocated chores before setting off for school. Millie had no say in the matter and simply did as she was told by her domineering husband.

Hope was overjoyed on being told the good news. Her dream of having an education had at last been realised, thanks to Grandma Florence. Hope immediately selected the best-looking hand of bananas from the garden and presented it to Grandma Florence in appreciation.

SCHOOL DAYS

There was no specific age or protocol for starting school at the time. Children simply presented themselves and gave their name to the headmaster, who entered it onto the school register. All new arrivals were placed in the lowest ability group, but were upgraded in relation to their progress and potential.

Hope was ten years old when she entered the school house for the very first time. She had waved to her family, including Grandma Florence, as they stood and watched her set off on her first school day. No other member of the family had previously attended school and both Millie and Tom were quietly sceptical. But Florence was delighted and beamed with pride.

The journey to school was hot and hazardous, but undaunted and proudly wearing her new frock, Hope jogged and skidded barefooted across muddy, hilly and steep tree-lined pathways, clutching her slate and chalk. She also carried a slice of breadfruit wrapped in a large leaf to be eaten during the lunch break. Hope was joined on the way by various children from other communities who had been fortunate enough to receive the opportunity of having an elementary education. Hope would undertake the school journey every day during term time for four short years.

The Catholic school house in St David's was built in 1818. The teaching was elementary and based on reading, writing and arithmetic. Students were divided into groups that were primarily dependent on ability.

The school day began with the chiming of bells. Everyone trooped into the school house and stood as the register was called by the Headmaster. A hymn was bellowed by pupils and teachers alike before the children were permitted to sit for lessons. It was an age when teaching and learning methods involved repetitive, tuneful rhyming designed for memorising the basic principles of the three Rs.

The Headmaster sat sharp eyed in a chair on the stage or raised section at the front of the hall, menacingly clutching a large cane, while overseeing the different groups. Any child suspected of being disruptive or not paying attention would be promptly and sternly summoned to stand before the Headmaster for at least one stinging stroke of the rod on the palm of each hand.

It would not be long before Hope realised that the best way of avoiding the Headmaster's wrath was by not speaking unless being spoken to by the teacher and paying full attention at all times. Hope was enthusiastic about learning her numbers and also the alphabet in rhyme fashion along with other beginners during her first school term. She would progress to being taught to read and write by following instructions from the teacher, which often involved copying from the blackboard onto her slate. The children also learnt from shared copies of the Royal Reader, an educational text commonly used in schools of the period. A limited number of copies would be distributed among students and collected at the end of the lesson. The abilities and progression of pupils in reading, writing, comprehension, spelling and numbers were regularly tested.

A bell was rung at around 12 noon, signalling the lunch break. The children were by that time extremely hungry. Many would have had an early start and carried out various chores prior to leaving for school. And whatever food they carried with them would be quickly eaten while sitting in the school yard. Goblets containing drinking water were provided for the children and latrines containing buckets were regularly emptied by appointed female staff. The end of the lunch break was again signalled by the bell and the children returned to their separate class groups.

There was general relief when they heard the final bell indicating the end of the school day. Everyone stood and chanted the obligatory prayer, led by the Headmaster, prior to being 'let off'. The return journey home was always filled with fun and free-spirited abandonment. The children would chase each other, climb trees and snack on seasonal fruit. Others, particularly boys, argued in raised voices, squabbled and wrestled.

On arriving home, an exhilarated Hope would signal her return by shouting at the top of her voice: "Ar reach!" – before changing into ragged dress ready to do her mother'sbidding.

Encouraged by unfailing support from Grandma Florence, Hope did well. She passed all tests set by teachers to determine pupils' progress and was upgraded to higher classes. But Tom and Millie showed no interest and it remained a thorn in Tom's side that his daughter was attending school. He was ignorant of the benefits of education and was convinced that it was a complete waste of time.

Hope attended school for four short years, but at age 14 she received the honour of being the first member of her family to have successfully learnt reading, writing and arithmetic. Despite his initial scepticism, Tom reluctantly conceded that his girl had not done too badly after all. It had been a proud moment for the entire family.

Florence was particularly thrilled and took full credit for her grand-daughter's success : she took full credit for Hope's achievement and boasted to everyone in the community that it was she who persuaded Elias 'to make Tom sen de chile to school' in the first place; personally stitched all her school frocks; and even provided the required slate and chalk.

Florence had been instrumental in making sure that news of Hope's abilities was spread throughout the small community. She made it clear that her grand-daughter could be called upon to read or reply to any letter collected from the post office.

But tragedy struck just six months after Hope's educational achievement when Florence collapsed with a mystery illness. Despite being treated with the best herbal remedies, Florence died just three days after falling ill. She was just 50 years of age. The family and everyone in the close-knit community and beyond were shocked and saddened by the popular grandmother's untimely demise. Elias would survive his wife by just two years.

Hope was deeply affected by Florence's unexpected departure. Not only had she lost a beloved grandmother, but also her best friend and confidante.

Despite the devastating loss, time ticked by, and during the ensuing years Hope continued to use her literacy skills to assist others. But she never forgot that she would not have had the opportunity of an education without the assistance and continuous support of her dear departed grandmother.

Caribbean women: En route to market in the 1800s.

FOURTEEN AND UP

In those days, when girls reached the age of 14, they were declared 'big girls' and were required to shoulder a greater share of household duties and family responsibilities. Hope received additional tasks, including sharing the day-to-day management of the younger children and preparing produce for everyday use and also for selling at market. At the end of each week, Hope would accompany her mother on the long sweaty walk to Grenville. On their heads would be perched large baskets overflowing with produce intended to be sold for profit.

Hope was also tasked with washing the family's clothing and bedding in the river every Monday morning alongside other girls and women. It was not unusual, in those days, to see small girls actually washing items of clothing and afterwards sitting on their mother's lap and being breast fed.

Sunday remained the day Hope looked forward to. She loved putting on her one and only best dress and walking to and from Church with other young people. The youngsters were always happy and jovial. No-one seemed to be listening as they spoke at each other in loud voices, but their simultaneous hysterical laughter suggested that everyone had heard and was tickled by the same joke.

Groups of boys and girls would gather at the usual meeting point on Sunday afternoons. Spurred on by others, a boy might make a move towards a particular girl, but often risked being faced by a chorus of giggles and ridicule from the love interest and her group of girly friends.

Hope was 16 when she was first approached by 18-year-old Sam Polite. He had been secretly attracted to her for some time, but was always too shy to reveal his true feelings – although the bravado he displayed when he was among his peers may have suggested differently.

The cocky, self-assured male posturing of Sam and his contemporaries had the desired effect of gaining attention from girls. But unbeknown to the rest of the group, Sam cringed whenever one of them was rebuffed. He dreaded being so publicly rejected and decided to wait for an opportune moment before making his move.

Sam grabbed the moment when he crossed paths with Hope while on an errand. He impulsively stepped closely to Hope and whispered into her ear. "What yuh say?" asked Hope. "Ar say ar like yuh," repeated Sam in a louder whisper. Hope heard him this time, but said nothing. She was unsure of what her response should be. What did he mean? She thought and recalled that she had known Sam all her life. He lived on a neighbouring settlement and was quite friendly with her two brothers. Hope wondered whether they were related. Sam's mother was commonly known as Cousin Joanie, but various other adults in the locality were also called Cousin this or Cousin that.

The following Sunday, when groups of boys and girls gathered to watch a cricket match, Hope could sense Sam's gaze. She felt very self-conscious and made every effort to avoid him. Sam said nothing.

On the Monday morning, while carrying the family's laundry to a nearby river, Hope spotted Sam, followed by two goats attached to ropes. She knew instantly that the animals were being taken to fertile ground for feeding. Sam caught sight of Hope and shouted, "Ar go see yuh in de garden!" Hope shrugged her shoulders. She knew that she was expected to assist her father on the land after the washing was completed and that Sam was usually working on his own family's plot not too far away. "We go see," Hope thought.

Hope quite enjoyed meeting up with other girls and women on wash day. The group would engage in the latest gossip as they energetically rubbed and beat items of clothing clean with blocks of soap, on large stones that were permanently lodged in the water. Hope always made sure that stains were thoroughly removed from every piece of clothing and ready for inspection by her mother. Any vague shadows would result in the particular item being angrily thrown into mud by Millie, where it would have to be retrieved and washed spotless.

On returning from the river, Hope carefully spread the freshly washed laundry on low-hanging branches of trees to be scrutinised by Millie. If judged satisfactorily washed, the clean laundry would be dried in strong sunlight. After being given the nod of approval, Hope was relieved to be permitted to help herself to some of the cooked food from a large pot that had been simmering on a dying wood fire in the yard. But as she was about to sit on a stone to have her meal, Millie shouted harshly at her daughter: "Hurry up!" – and reminded Hope of her next scheduled task.

As instructed, Hope ate her food quickly and hurried to assist Pa Tom on the land. She was gripped with feelings of apprehension and her stomach churned as she remembered that Sam had said he would see her in the garden. She could not help being curious about Sam's intentions and wondered what he would say to her.

When Hope arrived on the family's plot, Pa Tom was busy digging up yams and potatoes. She also caught sight of Sam working a little distance away on his own family's plot. Without lifting his head, Tom told his daughter to pick up the provisions that he had already dug up, take them home and return quickly, as there was plenty more for her to do. Hope did as she was told and the afternoon was filled with reaping and gathering of crop. After some time, Pa Tom slowly stood up from his bending position and stretched his back. He had done enough for the day and returned to the house, leaving Hope to gather the remaining crop before coming home.

Suddenly Sam, barefooted and wearing just a rough-edged pair of short pants, was standing beside Hope as she loaded provision into a large sack. She pretended not to notice his presence and continued to hold her head down while carrying on with the task in hand.

Sam was not deterred and nervously reiterated his liking for Hope, before asking her to meet him under a named mango tree deep in the bush the following day after Pa Tom had left for home. Hope said nothing, but after Tom had left her side, various thoughts flooded her mind and she felt a little tingly as she assessed his overall appearance. Tom was a lean, dark-skinned lad of medium height with a dazzling smile. Hope shivered nervously as she contemplated their planned meeting.

The next day arrived in the blink of an eye and Hope found herself alone in the garden wondering whether or not she should join Sam under the named mango tree. But she was curious to hear what he had to say and soon after Pa Tom left the garden for home, Hope hurried to meet Sam. She was relieved that he was already there and waiting. "Ar glad yuh come." Sam beamed as he grabbed Hope's hand. The pair said very little to each other as they sat side by side beneath the tree. Sam grinned broadly and thought how lucky he was that Hope had actually met up with him. Hope felt somewhat embarrassed and kept her head bowed. After a short while the couple agreed to meet again, same place, same time, 'tomorrow'. They both knew that their meetings had to be brief if they were to avoid suspicion.

The connection between Hope and Sam developed as they continued to meet secretly, but Sunday was the day they were free to spend more time in each other's company. Hope could not help being warmed by Sam's loving words. She would melt in his tender embraces and glow with contented fulfilment.

It had been a happy period that was tinged with excitement as the loved-up couple maintained their secret liaisons. But all good things come to an end and without warning Hope began to feel nauseous, particularly on mornings, and often threw up in the bush. She was also alarmed that her regular monthly cycle had ceased.

Millie became aware that her daughter was unable to keep down her breakfast, which consisted mainly of fried breadfruit, cassava or corn porridge, followed by a cup of hot 'cocoa tea'. Millie was also concerned that she had not noticed signs of Hope having a period for some time.

Millie picked up on the signs and, convinced that her girl was with child, confronted her with questions, "Yuh dae wid ar boy? Ar wan' to no hu!" Hope responded by bursting into uncontrollable tears, but Millie was unsympathetic. She ordered Hope to fetch a rod to deliver the thrashing that would be a proper reason for crying. At that point, Hope opened up and tearfully revealed her secret meetings with Sam.

Shocked and flabbergasted, Millie took Hope by the hand, marched purposefully to Sam's yard, where his mother, Cousin Joanie, was sitting shelling peas, and angrily declared that Hope was expecting Sam's child.

Cousin Joanie's hands fell motionlessly in the bowl of peas that lay on her lap and listened intently as she was told about the young couple's secret romance.

Joanie, a single mother of several children fathered by different men, responded in a matter-of-fact fashion which appeared to suggest that the pregnancy was just an inevitable part of life; but she pledged to go along with any decision made by Millie's husband, Tom. Both women were aware that they really had very little say in the matter and that everything depended on Tom.

Millie made sure that the younger children were out of the way by the time their father returned from the garden. After Tom had eaten his dinner and was in a relaxed mood, Millie hesitantly revealed their daughter's predicament. All the while, Hope sat quietly and nervously under the shade of a nearby tree, anxiously anticipating Pa Tom's response.

Tom's outraged reaction had not been unexpected. He said nothing to Hope, but told Millie that she must find Sam and bring him to the yard immediately! Cousin Joanie had by then spoken to her son and his decision was made prior to being summoned to face the music. And before Tom was able to utter a word, Sam grabbed the moment and quickly declared his wish to marry Hope. Tom and Millie were both taken by surprise, but Tom indicated his approval and acceptance of the young man's proposal by nodding slowly but purposefully. Hope, who was not too far away, had overheard Sam's expressed intentions and was delighted.

After Sam had left for home, Tom sat in the yard and quietly sucked on his pipe. He recalled the anger of his father-in-law Elias when he heard that Tom had been meeting secretly with Millie. It seemed that history had come full circle. Like Elias before him, Tom was disappointed to learn of his daughter's behaviour, but was happily satisfied that Sam was an honourable young man who intended to do right by his daughter.

THE MARRIED WOMAN

One month after the pregnancy became known, Sam and Hope, accompanied by close family members, walked to the Catholic Church in St David's, where the couple was pronounced Mr and Mrs Samuel Polite after taking their marriage vows.

The wedding party then returned to the yard surrounding the home of the bride's parents, where they were provided with a meal of corned pork and boiled provision, followed by sweet potato pudding and cupfuls of freshly made sorrel and ginger beer.

Sam and Hope began their married life in a two-room wooden shack that had been speedily constructed on a plot of land that was gifted to the couple by Pa Tom. Generous well-wishers provided the couple with gifts intended to provide a start to their new life together. These included young farm animals from their own meagre livestock, such as chickens, kid goats and piglets.

Honeymoon periods were unheard of in those days and the day after the wedding, Sam busily tended his recently acquired plot of land, while Hope carried out various housekeeping tasks. Although confident of the help and support that was readily available from relatives and also within the close-knit community, Sam, like many others of the era, was a proud man. He was determined to apply the hard labour that was necessary for being independent in providing for his young family.

In June 1863, five months after the marriage, Hope, by then 18 years of age, gave birth to her first daughter. The infant was christened Frances Margaret Polite but was soon being called Dee Dee, a name by which she would become commonly known.

Hope experienced no difficulty adjusting to her mothering role. After all, she had become accustomed to caring for children, having shared the task of looking after her own younger siblings.

Despite the responsibilities associated with being a wife and mother, which included working the land alongside her husband during the planting and reaping seasons, Hope received permission from Sam to continue using her literacy skills to assist with reading or replying to the occasional letter received by individuals who lived in their community. Having the ability and being given the opportunity to offer assistance to those who experienced reading difficulties provided for Hope a sense of vocational fulfilment and served to enhance personal feelings of self-satisfaction and worth. Hope was thankful that, though Sam was himself illiterate, he nonetheless demonstrated an awareness of the value of education and was supportive of his offspring being sent to school on a regular basis. It did not alter the fact that the couple and their family carried on a basic country lifestyle that mirrored cultural norms of the day.

Shortly after the birth of Dee Dee, Hope found herself pregnant for the second time.

The routines of daily life continued as one year followed the next and the day arrived when Hope woke to find that she had reached 29 years of age. She was at that stage married for twelve years and was heavily pregnant with her seventh child. During the intervening years, Sam had become increasingly controlling and Hope found herself following the footsteps of her mother and being trapped in an oppressive marital abyss. But while Ma Millie and many other long-suffering, downtrodden women stoically bore their marital cross, Hope grew restless and discontent and contemplated various ways of getting out of her situation.

About to enter her third decade, Hope dreaded the thought of ending her days without experiencing a less arduous lifestyle. She was convinced that she was destined for better in a foreign land. It was grandma's prophecy and she was always right. Hope often reflected on being told by Grandma

Florence that she should seek a better quality of life on the island of Trinidad when she became older. Florence wanted the best for her grand-daughter and Hope was determined that, by the Grace of God, she would one day turn grandma's dream for her into reality.

Hope at that point intended to do right by her husband and children and wondered whether a better life would indeed be guaranteed if the whole family emigrated. She finally decided to take the risk of cautiously broaching the subject with Sam on a Sunday afternoon when the children were out enjoying their separate pursuits.

On hearing his wife's suggestion, Sam, who had been quietly smoking his pipe, hit the roof. In his mind, Hope had overstepped the mark and needed to be put back in her place. Had she forgotten that she was a woman and had no right of expression or opinion? Sam was enraged. He felt that his status as the patriarch head of the family had been violated by his wife and such a thing could not be tolerated.

Most wives of the day were expected to honour the vow of obedience and had no right of opinion regarding life-changing family decisions. It was the accepted price for being granted the privilege of being taken as a wife. And a large number of husbands felt that their women should consider themselves 'lucky' they married them and be forever grateful and respectful.

Sam laid down the law by forcefully asserting that Hope must never again even consider making any suggestion regarding the family's future. Hope was saddened and disappointed by her husband's outburst. But his response provided insight into the reason Grandma Florence felt unable to have her say regarding the independent life options that had been available to newly freed slaves. It was indeed a paternalistic age in a community where men ruled and women in general were undervalued, disrespected and considered no more than commodities. But, far from breaking her spirit, Sam's harsh words only served to strengthen Hope's resolve.

She became resolute in her intention to be free from what she considered a long-suffering 'hellish' existence.

Hope had an idea. It involved secretly saving every half-penny of spare cash in a cloth purse, buried in soil under the mango tree that once witnessed her steamy relationship with Sam. She prayed each day that God would give her the strength and courage that was needed for carrying through a bold and daring endeavour, and begged forgiveness for even considering breaking her marriage vows by placing personal aspirations before her primary duties as wife and mother.

Hope knew that the children would be well cared for by their father, relatives and almost everyone in the community in her absence. She remained on course by reminding herself constantly of Grandma Florence's words: "Hope, yuh mus go in Trinidad. Yuh go have luk der."

At night time, while Sam snored loudly beside her, Hope would lay awake consumed with self-scrutiny. She often placed a hand firmly on her large bump in an attempt to calm the intermittent kicking of the child within her, before drifting into deep thought. Hope reasoned that she had attended school for four long years, successfully learnt to read and write, and in her view was an educated woman who deserved better. She had reached the end of her tether and was no longer prepared to continue her wearisome life. Hope was convinced that a bright future awaited her across the seas.

Daily routines of family life continued as usual, but all the while Hope was diligently saving a percentage of every penny earned on market days. She had been keenly aware that taking cash from the family's sale of nutmegs would be a risk too large to take, as that budget was being supervised and controlled exclusively by Sam.

It was not too long before the day arrived when the children were once more standing in the yard listening to agonising groans and gasps coming from the house. Sam was nowhere in sight as they waited anxiously to hear the cries that would signal the arrival of a new brother or sister.

Hope, assisted by her mother Millie, was about to give birth to her seventh baby.

The cries of the new arrival were met with cheers from the children. But the siblings knew that they were not allowed to enter the house until Grandma Millie gave the nod.

Within approximately thirty minutes, the children had been introduced to their new baby sister. Grandma Millie was on her way home and Dee Dee cradled the infant while Hope prepared dinner. It was not unusual for women in those days to carry out routine housekeeping tasks or even work the land, shortly after giving birth.

When the baby was just three weeks old, she was baptised into the Catholic faith and given the name May Ann Polite. Five months passed. Hope's secret planning had been completed and everything needed for undertaking a daring and high-risk operation was in place.

Hope surrendered willingly and with uncharacteristic fervour to her husband's conjugal demands, the night prior to the eventful day in 1875 when she would begin her painstakingly planned dauntless journey. It was the couple's final embrace.

While Sam slumbered deeply and contentedly, Hope, gripped with fear and apprehension, lay nervously awake, contemplating the right moment for taking the giant leap of faith that should lead to personal freedom. She prayed for strength, courage and fortitude.

It may have been just minutes after midnight when Hope steeled herself out of the family home while everyone was soundly asleep, including five-month-old May, who lay snugly in her arms.

The darkness of the night had been slightly lightened by a glimmering full moon and stars that twinkled across the skies. The temperature was cool and breezy. The only sounds were the buzzing of insects and the bustling of leaves.

Hope hurried to a specific mango tree and underneath retrieved a straw bag which contained a small lantern, a few items of clothing, a bottle of water, a large slice of breadfruit and a large number of coins that had been safely secured in a cloth purse.

Hope quickly proceeded to navigate her journey along familiar but hazardous pathways, stopping briefly to light the lantern that would further alleviate the blackness of the night en route to the island's capital, St George's. It was Hope's intention to be a long way from the parish of St David before the break of dawn, or 'fore day morning' as it was called in those days. She prayed continuously for the necessary stamina to remain resolute as she tackled the perilous journey with anxiety-filled steely determination. There were intermittent stops for rest and baby May was calmed and comforted on the go by being held securely and fed from the breast at regular intervals. It was only on reaching St Paul's, a suburb of St George's, before the crack of dawn, that Hope dared to think that her gallant endeavour might not have been undertaken in vain. She dropped to her knees in a prayer of thanksgiving and freshened at a clear-water stream before embarking on the last few miles to the island's harbour. She was heartened by the light that flickered at what in her mind appeared to be the end of a long black tunnel.

DISAPPEARED

Cocks could be heard loudly crowing in repetitive chorus up and down the island when Tom woke from a long and restful night's sleep. He stretched his arms and legs to their fullest, yawned loudly and made a sign of the cross before stepping out of bed. The children were also awake and on their knees as they chanted a familiar morning prayer. The night's bedding was afterwards scooped from the floor by 12-year-old Dee Dee and spread on the branches of a tree for airing. The younger siblings changed into ragged clothing and began carrying out routine tasks such as emptying the family's potty, fetching water from the stream, collecting fire wood and looking after the animals.

No alarm bells rang regarding Hope's absence as she would often take the baby to the river for an early bath before the rest of the family were awake. After relieving himself in the bush, Sam visited the river for his usual morning splash.

On returning home, Sam asked Dee Dee if she knew the whereabouts of her mother and was concerned to learn that none of the children had laid eyes on Hope that morning. He immediately decided that Dee Dee should begin preparing breakfast, which was usually coco tea and reheated leftovers from the previous night's dinner, while he searched for Hope.

Sam looked in bushes and searched the yards of relatives and friends, but there was no sign of Hope. News of Hope's disappearance quickly spread throughout the community and beyond, and people were genuinely worried. They formed into groups and scanned plantations and beaches while shouting her name. Others prayed for her safe return. Everyone assumed that 'baby May' was safe in the care of her mother, wherever that might be.

While residents in the community were searching or praying for her return, Hope was standing on the deck of a vessel en route to Trinidad, with little May in her arms. She watched tearfully and with a heavy heart as the land mass faded into the distance. Hope wondered whether she would ever again set foot on the island of her birth or even see her family again.

Suddenly, Hope's thoughts were interrupted by a comforting hand on her shoulder and she looked around to find a woman with a kindly face standing beside her. Speaking in sympathetic tones, the woman asked if all was well. Hope did not reply, but burst into tears.

After a while the sobs subsided and Hope found herself opening up to a complete stranger. She revealed the difficult circumstances which prompted the risky decision to seek a better quality of life in a foreign land as an independent woman. Hope revealed also that she had no contacts on the island of Trinidad and had no idea where she would find lodgings.

The kindly woman listened to Hope's story with amazement tinged with admiration. She had not previously heard of any female taking such courageous action and considered the younger woman extraordinarily brave. She decided there and then to do everything possible to help her. The stranger extended a hand and said that her name was Gladys. Gladys explained that she was Grenadian born but resided in Trinidad and had been visiting with relatives in the homeland. Gladys assured Hope that she and the baby would be more than welcome to stay at her family home in Diego Martin, Port of Spain, until she succeeded in finding work and a place of her own. Hope was also pledged assistance with looking after the baby if and when required.

Hope was overcome by Gladys' generous offer of accommodation and ongoing support and thanked her wholeheartedly. Any fears harboured by Hope of being alone and without refuge in a foreign land evaporated. She thanked God for dispatching a Good Samaritan at the most critical of moments.

Back home, the search for Hope continued and prayers for her safe return became increasingly desperate; but it was all to no avail. No sightings of Hope had been reported.

At the end of a harrowing and futile day, a lone middle-aged spinster in the community known as Miss Baptiste came forward and offered to care for the children in her own home pending their mother's return.

Grandpa Tom supported Sam's decision to accept Miss Baptiste's generous offer. Providing his grandchildren with food would not have been a problem, but there was no available space in his tiny shack for accommodating the siblings. Millie was silently supportive of her husband's decision. Even though the majority of grandmothers willingly cared for their grandchildren, Millie lacked energy. She was not in robust health and felt tired and worn down after many years of childbearing and hard work.

The days went by, but nothing was seen or heard of Hope and it became apparent that she had 'run away'. Everyone on the settlement and those beyond were either stunned or outraged. Hope's action was unthinkable. Never before had any woman in their community taken the bold step of abandoning her husband and children.

Hope's unprecedented action was a sensational and talked about phenomenon in a community where there was previously little ruffling of their slow-paced and accepted way of life. Women would get together by the river on wash days and in tones of awe and disbelief recount events and express opinions on the scandal that had rocked their settlement. The men adopted a cynical view of women whom they felt could not be trusted and became watchful of their movements. There were those who attempted preventive measures by threatening dire consequences should their women even think of following in the footsteps of Hope.

Various rumours were circulated and most believed was that Hope had left her family to set up home with an unknown man who lived on the island of Trinidad. Decorum was unheard of in the community in those days, and Sam found that he was often the open target of rebuke or condescension for failing to keep his wife 'in line'. And the siblings were subjected to regular taunting from their peers.

Sam's personal feelings alternated between disbelief, shock, humiliation, heartache and anger. He would lay awake at night trying to recall any signals or clues that Hope may have been planning to abandon the family. He could think of none. In fact, she had been most caring, compliant and submissive to his demands in the weeks leading to her disappearance. Sam would shake his head in bewilderment and disbelief and ask himself, 'How de woman could do somting like dat?' The idea that Hope's disappearance might have had anything to do with his unreasonable behaviour would not have crossed Sam's mind. All blame was placed fully on Hope, whom he cursed for being a wicked and evil woman for breaking their sacred vows.

Grandma Millie and other members of the extended family came to the conclusion that Hope had been led astray by the Devil. They prayed fervently for the redemption of her soul.

The siblings were teased mercilessly by other children for being abandoned. They were confused by Hope's absence, but relieved that they did not have to face her dreaded rages which, unaware to them, were often due to their father's mistreatment of her. It was nonetheless commonplace in those days that children were fearful of parents. The discipline regime required being at all times mindful of their behaviour in the presence of elders and although seen must not be heard.

A formal system of Welfare Services was not in existence in those days. It was the cultural norm that extended family members or interested members of the community would provide a home to children who had been orphaned or whose mother for whatever reason was unable to cope. It was on this basis that Miss Baptiste offered to care permanently for the siblings when it became apparent that Hope may not be returning home.

Miss Baptiste was a single woman with no children of her own. She lived in a neat three-room wooden dwelling and many in the community admired her 'big house'. They considered her privileged to be sleeping in a large four-poster bed and were in awe of her small drawing room crammed with mahogany furniture, including a cabinet filled with colourfully painted glasses and tureens that were made of the finest bone china. The contents of the house had been presented to Miss Baptiste's fore-fathers by their French Master when he returned to France after the island had been taken over by the British and were passed down the generations. But there were those who were dismissive of Miss Baptiste's possessions and expressed the view that without children a woman really had nothing.

Sam had no hesitation in accepting Miss Baptiste's offer to care for his children. He considered her a good and Godly woman and could think of no better mother-figure for his offspring. Sam was further reassured in the knowledge that the family would also receive support and assistance from relatives and the community at large.

Miss Baptiste also offered to take on Sam's laundry and prepare his meals. Sam presented himself at Miss Baptiste's yard every morning and evening without fail, where he received a plate of food accompanied by a cup of hot 'cocoa tea', coffee or whatever beverage was on offer.

Sam retained overall responsibility for his children and provided the family with food from the garden and money for purchasing material items when required. But he was a proud man and concealed the fact that he had been painfully embarrassed being deserted by his wife and had descended to being a 'laughing stock' in the community. Sam felt that his status as a man had been severely undermined and he became bitter and mistrustful of women. His evenings were spent sitting alone in the family shack, drowning his sorrows in a bottle of rum, before falling asleep in a drunken stupor. If his intention was to break the spirit of his wife when she dared to suggest emigration to Trinidad, the table had well and truly rebounded. Tom was now a humiliated and broken man.

Miss Baptiste, who always harboured the desire for a family of her own, felt that her prayers had at last been answered. She was grateful for being given the opportunity of raising the siblings. 'God works in mysterious ways, his wonders to perform,' she often said. Miss Baptiste was convinced that the events which led to the children being placed in her care had been pre-ordained.

Miss Baptiste made sure the siblings carried out their routine allocated chores to her satisfaction and used stern words to keep them in line. They were always well fed and, as directed by Sam, sent to school on a regular basis. Sunday continued to be the day that the siblings were free to engage in their separate interests.

Many months flew by and in an era when sturdily built curvaceous women were pleasing to the eye, fresh rumours were circulated that Hope had been seen in Trinidad 'looking nice and fat', and that she was working in a store in Port of Spain. The siblings were by that time fully adjusted into the care of Miss Baptiste, whom they now called 'Cousin B'.

Dee Dee in particular looked up to Cousin B. She admired her colourful full-skirted frocks and matching turbans; the way she walked, with her head held high, and her compassionate nature. Dee Dee often peered through the glass cabinet filled with colourful glasses, china and ornaments and dreamt of one day owning a large house in which there would be a similar beautifully filled cabinet.

Dee Dee and her siblings received cups of brewed herbs commonly known as 'bush tea' whenever they were unwell. Specific herbs were, at that time, regularly used for treating various minor ailments such as coughs, colds, fevers, headaches and stomach upset.

SIGNIFICANT EVENTS 1876 AND 1877

In April 1876, Cousin B and Sam were alarmed when one of the siblings developed a raging fever that was not calmed by tried and tested remedies. The child was taken to see the parish Physician, Dr William Wells. Following examination, liquid medication was prescribed, to be taken three times a day, and the doctor advised Cousin B to make sure that the patient rested and received frequent cool drinks of water and other fluids.

Ordinary folk living in communities throughout the parish of St David's were not aware that Doctor Wells, who lived with his family in a large house at the top of a long pathway, was also a Political Speaker at the House of Representatives in St George's. And he had been the sole objector when, on 9th February 1876, a vote was taken and passed to petition the Queen to make Grenada a Crown Colony.

Dr Wells protested that the vote removed the rights of Grenadians to have a say in the passing of laws by which they were governed. But it was, in reality, a period when only the white elite and a few merchants and professionals of mixed-race heritage participated in the electoral process and laws passed were mainly for their benefit.

Grenada was declared a Crown Colony on 3rd December 1877. It meant that Britain controlled the affairs of the island directly and the implementation of Laws passed in Britain was the responsibility of the Governor-in-Chief and his Legislative Council.

Cousin B and many others in the community were aware of the opening of St Joseph's Convent in the town of St George in 1877. It had been the first secondary school for girls on the island, but ordinary people throughout Grenada knew well that the fee-paying education provided by the Convent was beyond their reach and accessible only to the daughters of the wealthy elite.

KEYHOLE VIEW OF A FAMILY, 1876-1883

For one family who lived in the Black Forest of Boca in the parish of St George, 1876 was marked by the birth of an infant boy. The child was one of three brothers and one sister and was given the name William Thomas Radix.

Mr and Mrs Radix, better known as Papee and Tant Cecae by their offspring, relatives and friends, had been the children of freed slaves who decided to accept the option of independent living in the homeland. The couple's respective fore-bears were among pioneers of settlement dwellers on rented or purchased land in their particular parish. And their life experiences mirrored those who lived in similar communities across the island.

Papee was a hardworking and enterprising man who had made good. He owned the Radix estates, in those days pronounced Radee, which yielded substantial quantities of nutmeg. The family lived in a four-room wooden house with an adjoining kitchen. A latrine was constructed at the bottom of the garden and there were stables for the family-owned horses.

Papee was quiet and serious. A reclusive by nature, he had very few friends, if any, and was a man of not many words who enjoyed his own company. Papee's favourite pastime was sitting on his rocking chair in a secluded part of the yard and smoking a large pipe. He would at the same time thoughtfully turn the pages of an encyclopaedia, which was his prized possession; or twirl an atlas that was precariously perched on its axle, while observing the countries and continents of the world. He marvelled at the fact that Grenada was a mere dot, even in comparison with other islands.

Tant Cecae was opposite in character. She was an outgoing and sociable woman who liked the company of friends and loved to engage in local gossip. In private moments, Tant Cecae often fretted about Papee's detached and uncommunicative manner.

Any attempt to initiate dialogue with her husband would be met with a short and abrupt response, or even coldly ignored. Papee was hardworking and reliably responsible and Tant Cecae received free rein within the household. Unlike many husbands of the period, Papee was not verbally demanding, but his silent methods of controlling and keeping his wife in her place were no less effective and most certainly emotionally and psychologically painful. Despite being one of a minority of privileged women who was not required to work the land, Tant Cecae often lamented on being a lonely and unhappy wife whose life revolved mainly around her children.

Papee also distanced himself from his offspring and rarely spoke to them. In his view they were part of the household and under the domain of their mother. But Papee desired the best opportunities for his children. He had attended school and was keenly aware of the value of education.

William, who had been a happy and engaging baby, developed into a boisterous and precocious toddler with an impressive grasp of language. William began attending school with his older siblings when he was just four years old and his favourite subject at that stage was play. But he would soon exhibit an enthusiasm for learning and was the first child in his class to learn the alphabet by heart. By the age of six, William knew his times tables and was able to add and subtract small numbers.

Although Papee never showed it, he was proud of his bright and charismatic youngest son. Both parents believed that their boy was special and destined for great things. The siblings loved their bright and delightful little brother and did not mind that he received few chores and was allowed to indulge in his love of play.

The family was shocked and bereft when suddenly and unexpectedly, Papee collapsed and died in his rocking chair while smoking on his favourite pipe. William was just seven years old. Regrettably, Papee was not destined to see what fate had in store for his beloved little boy.

GROWING UP IN THE 1870s AND 1880s

During the 1870s and 1880s, Dee Dee and her siblings were being raised on their humble settlement by their substitute mother, Cousin B. Dee Dee had been taken out of school altogether in 1876 after demonstrating to her proud father that she was able to read the letter collected from the Post Office by a family friend. His girl had done well and Sam could think of no further reason why 13-year-old Dee Dee should continue at school. From that point onwards, Dee Dee worked alongside Cousin B as they carried out day-to-day routines. The pair developed a close and friendly relationship and would often be engaged in breaking gossip.

Around 5 am one morning, as Cousin B and the children were stirring from their beds, a familiar voice was heard calling out for water. Dee Dee was instructed by Cousin B to pour a cup of water from the jug that was standing on the table and hand it to the man standing in the yard. He was a well-known member of the community.

Later that morning, as Cousin B and Dee Dee washed clothes in a nearby river, Cousin B paused, lifted her petticoat and revealed a large bruise on her left thigh. She told Dee Dee that the bruise was evidence that blood had been 'sucked' from her veins by a 'Lig-ah-rou' which entered the house by flying through the keyhole during the night.

Cousin B may not have been aware that the term 'Lig-ah-rou' was derived from the French Creole word Loup-Garou, the English equivalent of Werewolf; but she insisted that the morning visitor was without doubt a lig-ah-rou and that he had feasted on her blood while she slept. Cousin B based her belief on the fact that the individual had appeared at the house asking for water and that it was the standard request from Lig-ah-rous the morning after the night the invasively evil act had been committed. Dee Dee was not unaware of the supernatural. It was a cultural belief that spirits, known also as zombies, mingled within communities and recounting real or imagined ghostly tales was a regular occurrence. But she was nonetheless shocked and horrified and unable to fathom how a normally friendly and kindly gentleman who attended Church every Sunday could suddenly change into an evil blood-thirsty spirit.

That night, Dee Dee lay nervously beside her siblings on their bed of rags on the floor and listened intensely for any unusual noises that might indicate the return of the Lig-ah-rou. But nothing was heard, apart from the buzzing of insects and trees that bustled in the wind. There seemed to be no further visits from the unwelcome guest, but Dee Dee remained vigilant and, gripped with panic, would flee in the opposite direction whenever she came across the alleged Lig-ah-rou in human form.

One year followed the next and all too soon it was 1883. Dee Dee was now a slightly built, dark skinned young lady entering her 20th year. It was a happy and exciting period in Dee Dee's life and she harboured the feeling of being destined for something unusually wonderful that year. Dee Dee had been enjoying secret meetings in the bush or by the bay with Simon Telesford. Simon, a short and stocky, light skinned man, was 14 years Dee Dee's senior with an 11-year-old daughter known as Da Da from a previous relationship. Simon was Dee Dee's first love and she often dreamt of marrying him one day.

One afternoon a voice could be heard calling from a distance: "Miss Baptiste! Miss Baptiste!" Cousin B hurried to the yard and shouted back, "Look me here!" The children were curious. They stood together behind Cousin B as the stranger appeared and abruptly dropped a box he had been carrying onto the ground. He introduced himself as McGuire from Sauteurs and explained that he had met Miss Hope while visiting relatives in Trinidad and she asked him to deliver the parcel. Cousin B expressed her gratitude and provided McGuire with a dish of a freshly prepared meal and a large cup of cool lime juice sweetened with several scoops of wet sugar, before bidding him goodbye.

The children excitedly peered down and waited anxiously as Cousin B carefully opened the box and began to pull out a variety of items, including yards of colourful material, cookies and candy. The parcel also contained a letter which Cousin B passed to Dee Dee. It had been written by Hope and everyone listened carefully as Dee Dee, in a loud voice, read the contents of the letter to them. Hope wrote that she missed her family and prayed for them every day. The letter ended with a plea for a visit from the children. The siblings were overjoyed. It was the first time they had heard from their mother or received anything from her since her unexpected departure. They laughed, clapped, jumped up and down and ran gleefully around the yard.

Suddenly, everyone stopped in their tracks as, above the hullabaloo, the distinctive sharp tones of Cousin B could be heard calling for silence. In those days and in their community children were only permitted to be freely jovial on Sundays or special holidays. And the siblings were suddenly reminded that they had overstepped the mark. They were ordered back to their chores, but Cousin B was not without compassion and said that they would receive cookies and candy after the work had been completed to her satisfaction. It was a wonderful incentive. The children made sure that their separate tasks were carried out to perfection and were not disappointed. Each child received the promised treat and the day ended on a very happy note.

It was Cousin B's opinion that, at aged 20 and 18 respectively, Dee Dee and her brother Mark were old enough to make the trip. "Yuh wanna go an' see yuh muda she asked Dee Dee. "Yes, Cousin B," Dee Dee replied, as she attempted to conceal her excitement. "Ar go ask yuh farder," Cousin B said.

Sam was taken by surprise when he heard from Cousin B that Hope had sent a parcel to the children and requested a visit from them. He was immediately gripped by mixed emotions that churned his stomach. But Sam had mellowed a little over the years and, in keeping with being slightly more reasonable and considerate, shrugged his shoulders and declared that if Dee Dee and Mark wished to visit their mother, he would provide the necessary funds for the trip.

News that Hope had sent her family a large package and Dee Dee and Mark would be visiting their mother in Trinidad spread like wildfire; and memories of the scandalous event that rocked the sleepy community in 1875 were recounted and embellished.

Dee Dee wrote and posted a letter informing Hope of the planned trip, while Cousin B arranged for Dee Dee and Mark to be measured for new outfits to be made from material received from their mother.

Dee Dee and Simon got together deep in the bush for an emotional goodbye embrace the day prior to leaving for Trinidad. On the following morning, Dee Dee and Mark, dressed in their brand new outfits and newly purchased boots, set off on the long walk to St George's harbour. They carried straw bags containing personal items of clothing and a little food and water. Cousin B put together small packets of herbs, spices, cocoa and home-made guava and coconut candies that were to be passed on to Hope.

The children were allowed to walk with their older brother and sister until they reached the main path. The siblings parted company with the words 'bring somting back far us – eh?' ringing in the ears of Dee Dee and Mark.

On arrival at the harbour in St George's, Dee Dee paid the fare before jostling with many others onto a crowded boat en route to Trinidad. The seas were calm as the vessel cruised during the beginning of the journey. Dee Dee and Mark held on to the sides as they stood on deck and stared at the shrinking coastlines and beyond until the island was completely out of view.

After a while they sat on the floor and Mark was soon asleep with his head slumped forward. Dee Dee remained wide-eyed and consumed with thoughts of the changes that had occurred within the family following the disappearance of their mother. She was just a child at the time, but had since grown into a young woman. Dee Dee wondered whether mother and daughter would recognise each other after so many years.

Dee Dee was not affected by the hustle and bustle of passengers who were constantly on the move or spoke in loud voices, but was increasingly irritated by the noise of the engine, sickened by its pungent fumes and dizzied from the turbulent movements of the boat. Dee Dee sat closely to Mark, placed her head on his shoulder and quietly prayed, 'Jesus, Mary and Joseph, help me.' She was nauseous, her head throbbed and she would periodically stagger to the edge of the boat and throw up into the sea.

Mark snored lightly, oblivious to everything that was going on around him. It had been an early start and a long tedious walk over hilly and rugged terrain to St George's harbour and he was exhausted.

THE TRINIDAD EXPERIENCE

After what seemed like an eternity, the coastlines of Trinidad finally came into view. Dee Dee heaved a sigh of relief and made a sign of the cross as the boat eventually cruised into the pier and docked.

"Wake up! Wake up!" Dee Dee said urgently, as she shook Mark awake. "We reach! We reach!" she cried. "Arready?" Mark replied drowsily, as he wiped the sleep from his eyes. "Dar was quick! But ar enjoy de ride – it was reel nice.' Mark had slept soundly during the turbulent journey, but Dee Dee lacked the energy or will to tell him about her torturous experience.

The siblings straightened their clothes before following the passengers as they disembarked and eventually found themselves in the midst of a bustling port. Dee Dee and Mark walked around until they found a fairly quiet spot and waited anxiously and expectantly for their mother to appear. It was not too long before they saw a short, plump and buxom brown-skinned woman, with beads of perspiration trickling down her face, waddling breathlessly towards them with outstretched chunky arms. "Look how all yuh ger big," she screamed ecstatically as she enveloped the siblings into her arms and gushed, "Yuh dor remember me? I is all yuh muda." Dee Dee and Mark were taken by surprise and a little stiff in their response. They had never before received demonstrative affection from their mother. She seemed very different from the woman they remembered her to be. Following the warm welcome, brother and sister were taken to Hope's rented home in Diego Martin, Port of Spain.

Dee Dee and Mark were happy to meet their pretty 8-year-old sister May, who was just a baby when they last saw her; but were surprised that their mother and sister occupied just one large room in a shared house with communal use of a boarded outdoor latrine.

Hope was delighted with the simple gifts derived from natural sources and containing distinctive fragrances so reminiscent of home. But Dee Dee and Mark did not have to wait too long before being dished up large plates of rice served with corned beef seasoned with chilli peppers, onions and tomatoes. They had never before received such a meal or seen such large portions of rice and meat on individual plates. It seemed unbelievable and they gazed wide-eyed at the food, unsure whether or not it was theirs to eat. They were unexpectedly jolted out of uncertainty by their mother's voice directing them to, "Eat up all yuh food! Eat all yuh food!" It was the cue they were waiting for and the siblings immediately picked up their spoons and within a very short time the delicious meal had been consumed.

Hope was eager to receive news of the family back home and the pair was taken aback by the willingness of their mother to converse with them. They recalled that she spoke to her offspring only when they were being reprimanded or ordered to carry out specific tasks. But Dee Dee and Mark assured their mother that everyone was well and life was continuing as normal. Hope was particularly pleased to hear that the children she left behind had been taken in by Miss Baptiste, who did her best for them, and that they all attended school. Hope knew Miss Baptiste well and remembered stopping by her yard for little chats. She considered Miss Baptiste a pleasant and upstanding woman and thanked God that the siblings had been placed in her care.

Hope did not explain to Dee Dee and Mark her reasons for deserting the family, but revealed that, after arriving in Port of Spain, she stayed with a lady called Gladys, who had befriended her on the boat to Trinidad. Gladys and her family were very helpful and supportive. They assisted Hope with finding work, a place to live and were always willing to look after May whenever necessary. Hope went on to say that she missed the family back home, but Trinidad had been good to her. She had found herself a 'good' job in a store in town and tried to save as much money as possible. But Hope did not disclose that she had successfully fulfilled her dream of a better life or that Grandma Florence's prediction that she would be 'lucky' in Trinidad had become a reality. Hope now fostered a keen sense of liberation and felt she had escaped a life sentence. She had no intention of ever returning to the homeland and risk being recaptured. Hope's newly established independence had become one of her most treasured possessions.

Hope's boss at work had generously allowed her time off when she told him of the planned visit from her children. And while May was at school, Dee Dee and Mark were shown around town and treated to curried snacks sold from roadside stalls. The siblings were particularly overawed by the large numbers of people of different races and cultures, and the general hustle, bustle and vibrancy of the city. Mark was hugely impressed by fashionable young men swaggering in dungarees and broad-brimmed hats. He pictured himself similarly dressed and showing off to the lads back home. Dee Dee admired the ladies in their colourful frocks, matching turbans, large earrings and jingling gold bangles. She loved visiting the various stores and was struck by the variety of goods displayed. Dee Dee was particularly drawn to the beautiful jewellery and secretly wished for a pair of thick gold bracelets.

Despite being happily settled in her new life as an independent woman, Hope felt unable to recover from the guilt associated with abandoning her family. She prayed every day that God would forgive her for breaking her marriage vows. But she felt that liberation had transformed her into a better-natured and more considerate woman. Hope was overjoyed that Dee Dee and Mark had been permitted to visit her and saw it as an opportunity to make amends. She lavished attention and affection on the siblings during their short stay with her and proudly introduced them to her friends, including Gladys and her family. But Hope had a surprise in store. The siblings were taken on a special shopping trip on the day prior to their return journey home and invited to purchase any item of their choosing. Dee Dee and Mark already knew what they wanted and were ecstatic that their separate secret wishes were about to be realised.

Dee Dee and Mark's first vacation abroad had been an enjoyable and enlightening experience for them both, but, unbeknown to her mother and brother, Dee Dee was plagued by recurrent feelings of un-wellness throughout the holiday. She was convinced that the condition had been triggered by the turbulent boat journey and only persisted because of the intense heat. Dee Dee felt certain that she would be better after returning to the settlement, where the environment was warm and breezy during the day and comfortably cool at night.

It seemed that within a heart beat the holiday had come to an end. The siblings were sad to leave their mother, whom they now considered 'lovely', but very much looked forward to being back on familiar territory. Mark could hardly wait to show off his new fashionable outfit. Dee Dee found it hard to resist lifting her hands in admiration of the thick gold bracelet that adorned each wrist. Brother and sister were exceedingly happy with their chosen gifts, but they also carried boxes filled with presents from Hope for the folk back home.

There were hugs and kisses between the siblings and their mother as they bade her goodbye prior to boarding the boat for the return journey home. Hope asked the pair to convey her love and best wishes to the family and promised to keep in touch. But 18 long years would elapse before Dee Dee and her mother were destined to meet again.

BACK HOME

Dee Dee boarded the vessel secretly hoping and praying that the return trip would be less harrowing, but her prayers were only partly answered. Even though the seas were calm, there was no reprieve from the noisy engine, unpleasant odour and sea sickness. Needless to say, Mark remained in blissful oblivion during the entire passage. Dee Dee felt drained and fragile and was anxious to disembark when the vessel eventually docked on the pier in St George's. Mark, on the other hand, felt refreshed and rejuvenated at the end of what was for him a pleasant and restful journey.

After securing boxes on each other's heads, Dee Dee and Mark set off on the exhaustive walk to St David's. It was a hot day with intermittent heavy downpours and the pair stopped at various times to rest or shelter from the showers. Both Dee Dee and Mark were relieved when they finally entered Cousin B's yard and in unison called out: "We reach! We reach!" The younger siblings ran towards them, squeaking excitedly: "Wat all yuh bring? Wat all yuh bring?" Within minutes everyone had been alerted to Dee Dee and Mark's return and the yard was filled with inquisitive relatives and friends, eager and anxious to hear news of Hope. Dee Dee felt a compelling desire to put an end to the persistent speculation and rumour that her mother was with a man in Trinidad. She made it clear that Hope had found a 'good job' working in a store in Port of Spain and was interested only in saving as much of her earnings as possible, and making sure that young May was being properly cared for and attending school on a regular basis. This was at a time when only privileged or educated Grenadians were offered jobs as Sales Assistants in retail outlets in St George's town, and everyone was duly impressed on hearing that Hope had done so well. Grandma Millie, on the other hand, was not particularly surprised and in no uncertain terms refreshed the memories of those present by asserting that her daughter was an educated woman who, unlike many of them, had been to school, successfully learnt reading, writing and arithmetic and was well qualified to work in a store. There followed unanimous mutterings of acknowledgment and simultaneous nodding of heads.

Everyone moved forward and peered down inquisitively as Cousin B and Grandma Millie opened the boxes sent by Hope. And there were sounds of amazement as the contents were displayed. The people had never before seen such a variety of items at any one time and included boots in different sizes, ready-made garments, neckties, slates, chalk, pencils, cheese, biscuits and tins of corned beef. Cousin B and Grandma Millie made sure that everyone was given a little something. The children were thrilled with their separate gifts and gleefully clapped and cheered. Despite being delighted with a pair of laced boots which fitted perfectly, Sam was struck by a fresh attack of emotional turmoil. But it had essentially been an eye-opening moment, which indicated that Hope had indeed found relative prosperity and a better quality of life in the land of comparative opportunity.

On the Sunday following their return home, the siblings embarked on a leisurely but treacherous journey to Church dressed in their new outfits. Mark wore his trendy bright blue dungarees with laced boots and a broad-brimmed hat secured with a string on either side loosely tied under his chin. He emulated his Trinidadian contemporaries by swaggering and posturing in front of a bare-footed audience in simple shirts and short pants.

Dee Dee and Simon had previously arranged to meet up on that very Sunday afternoon. The couple missed each other immensely. They had been apart for two long weeks and could hardly wait to be alone together in their favourite secluded spot in the bush. So while Mark was once again showing off his fashionable attire to a mesmerised group of boys and girls, Dee Dee and Simon stole away for some private time together. Dee Dee presented her man with a hat extracted from a parcel sent by Hope. Simon was delighted with his gift and the couple's romance was re-ignited with an interlude of intense passion.

The weeks immediately following Dee Dee's return home had been difficult due to persistent feelings of nausea and lethargy. In spite of being continuously unwell, Dee Dee soldiered on with routine tasks. Cousin B had not been aware of Dee Dee's condition when she revealed that Pa Sam had decided to pay for Dee Dee to receive sewing lessons from a skilled seamstress in the locality. Dee Dee was very happy and somewhat relieved. She couldn't help but think that spending time 'learning to sew' would provide a welcome break from tedious chores.

A SECRET IS REVEALED

A close bond had developed between Dee Dee and Cousin B and the pair confided in each other their innermost thoughts and concerns. One Saturday morning, as the women walked side by side to market with baskets of produce carefully balanced on their heads, Dee Dee disclosed that she had been feeling poorly for some time and had missed two periods. Cousin B immediately had a suspicion, which she tested by asking if Dee Dee had been seeing a boy. It was an alarming question for Dee Dee, but she felt cornered and decided to confess her association with Simon Telesford. Cousin B nodded repeatedly as Dee Dee spoke. There was no doubting that her initial suspicion had been proven. She declared that Dee Dee was with child and Pa Sam would have to be told. Cousin B also warned that Dee Dee should have no further contact with Simon until Sam had made a decision on the matter.

Sam was hurt and disappointed when he heard from Cousin B that his eldest daughter may be expecting Simon Telesford's baby. He went to Simon's house bright and early the very next day, informed him of Dee Dee's condition and demanded to know what his intentions were. Simon scratched his head as he thought of a reply. He admitted eventually to having a secret association with Dee Dee and pledged that he would be a supportive father to their child. But Sam was floored when, 'bold as brass', Simon added that he had no intention of marrying Dee Dee or anyone else for that matter. Sam responded angrily. He accused Simon of being nothing but a 'piece of nastiness' and emphasised his deeply held conviction that young people 'nowadays' had no 'Rispek!'

That night, Sam Polite tossed and turned restlessly in his bed. He agonised about Dee Dee's situation and was outraged that Simon Telesford had no intention of making an honest woman of his daughter. Sam recollected being in a similar position many years previously and that he could not even have 'dreamed' of being so disrespectful to 'Mr Tom'. He shook his head despondently and wondered what the world was coming to 'today'! Sam also cast his mind back to the time when Hope just upped and left the family. It was a 'sore' point for him, but he had done the best he could for the children. Sam reasoned that he worked hard on the land and made sure they had plenty of food 'to eat'. But their day-to-day upbringing had been left in the hands of the kindly Cousin B, while he spent the majority of his spare time drinking rum and drowning his sorrows. Having become somewhat of a more reasonable man in recent years, Sam regretted not being more watchful of his daughter's movements. He vowed to make it up to her by taking full responsibility for the expected grandchild.

The next morning, Sam told Cousin B and Grandma Millie of the outcome of his talk with Simon. The women were equally shocked and angry and backed Sam's decision that Dee Dee must no longer 'waste time' with Simon.

Grandma Millie's anger simmered and she was determined to reap revenge. She decided on a plan and put it into action the very next week. Simon had been standing in his yard at the break of dawn filling his lungs with the fresh morning air, when he was suddenly and unexpectedly confronted by Millie. He opened his mouth to express a greeting, but was gagged and blinded by the rush of an odorous liquid and he spluttered furiously as the rancid solution seeped into his gaping mouth. Millie had purposefully tipped a chamber pot brimming with stale urine over Simon's head and without uttering a word marched off with a smug and satisfied expression on her face. Drenched and stunned, Simon was left speechless and rooted to the spot. He wondered whether 'the woman' had gone 'mad'.

News of the incident was quickly picked up and passed around the community; a wave of spiced gossip followed and Simon found himself the subject of various versions of a hilariously exaggerated joke. Millie could not be more pleased. The revenge reaped on behalf of her grand-daughter had indeed been sweet.

Meanwhile, Dee Dee was heartbroken. She felt that she had been deceived by the man she loved and whom she thought loved her in return. He had always sworn love for her whenever they were together in the bush. Dee Dee was bewildered and wondered whether she had done anything wrong. She tried to think of any warning signs and recalled that Simon always insisted on keeping their relationship secret. Dee Dee shrugged her shoulders. She decided that she had been naive and blinded by love and could do nothing but accept the consequences.

Like many other young women in the community, Dee Dee was resigned to her fate. But it was compounded by Cousin B, who asserted that Dee Dee did not have 'luck' like her mother and grandmother, whose partners had married them when they also fell pregnant at a young age. Cousin B was nevertheless a caring and empathetic woman. She decided that Dee Dee would no longer sleep on the floor with the younger children and could instead share her four-poster bed. Dee Dee was delighted. It would be her first experience of lying on a proper bed.

The following five months proved difficult for Dee Dee. Pregnancy was not considered an illness or excuse for not undertaking daily chores. Dee Dee carried on with the required work routines, despite having little appetite and being constantly weary. She looked forward to the respite of weekly sewing classes and restful nights in a comfortable bed.

Dee Dee was working the land alongside her father when she was suddenly gripped by surging pain in her belly. She did not complain and carried on working, despite the increasing frequency and intensity of her discomfort. After some time Sam decided to break for lunch, but had not noticed that his heavily pregnant daughter was bent over and struggling to walk. On arrival home, Dee Dee's distress was immediately spotted by Cousin B, who led her indoors and into bed. Dee Dee refused food and was only able to sip cool water. Sam fetched Gandma Millie, before returning to the land, and within hours Millie found herself assisting with the delivery of her very first great-grandchild.

Dee Dee gave birth to a healthy and beautiful baby on 25th October 1883. The infant, named Catherine Angelina Telesford, was Dee Dee's first daughter and Hope's first grand-daughter.

A FAMILY REVISITED

At the time of Catherine's birth, William Radix, who lived with his family many miles away in the Black Forest of Boca, was aged seven and had already started having private tuition. William's exceptional progress had been noted at the elementary school house he attended and brought to the attention of the Parish Priest. The Priest, commonly known as Father, felt that William should benefit from receiving access to a wider curriculum.

Father approached William's mother, Tant Cecae with the idea. He assured her that he would deliver additional tuition to William for one hour on two afternoons each week after school, if she agreed to the proposal. Tant Cecae was delighted and did not hesitate to give her seal of approval. No other child in their community had been known to have received such an opportunity and the entire family was proud of William's good fortune. Tant Cecae gave thanks to God for giving her this 'special boy'. She regretted that Papee had not lived long enough to witness their son's educational progression.

William would continue to receive private tuition from Father over the years and was an enthusiastic and hard-working student. As he grew older, William's interest in literature was awakened by being granted unlimited access to the various publications that were tightly slotted into place on crammed book shelves in his tutor's congested little Study.

Apart from using the family's encyclopaedia as a point of reference, access to books had been limited to Royal Readers, the educational text commonly used in schools of the day. Published in Scotland, Royal Readers were graded from Standard One to Standard Five and contained a variety of educational themes such as English grammar, English history and general knowledge. William was thrilled to have been allowed the freedom to select and peruse any book of interest. Introduction to literature proved profoundly beneficial to young William's academic development. And emulation of his mentor's diction was affirmation to the impactful influence of the priest's intervention during a formative and impressionable stage in William's life.

Despite the comparatively privileged education he received, William remained popular among his peers. He enjoyed joining them for a game of cricket at weekends, even though they teased and mimicked his 'funny' accent; but William refused to be intimidated. He remained focused on his studies and the encouragement and support received from his family never faltered.

Meanwhile, Tant Cecae was struggling to cope with the responsibilities associated with her late husband's estates. She would eventually sell off the excesses and retain what was deemed sufficient and manageable for ensuring the family's livelihood.

CAMPAIGNING BEGINS

Many ordinary folk living in rural communities may not have been aware of William Galway Donovan. In 1883, Donovan, who was of Irish and African descent, began a campaign for the removal of Crown Colony in Grenada. Under Crown Colony the island's affairs were directly controlled by Britain and the laws by which the people were being governed were passed in the British Parliament.

Donovan, along with 18 others, submitted to the Crossman Commission a memorandum which expressed the strongest objections to Crown Colony. Donovan used the *Grenada People*, a newspaper he owned and edited, as a voice for his vigorous campaign against the social and political injustices of the day. Its daily headlines carried the boldly printed slogan, 'A NAKED FREED MAN IS BETTER THAN A GILDED SLAVE'. Donovan's crusade was relentless and, by 1885, those who originally welcomed a Crown Colony Government were wholeheartedly against it. Eleven years previously, in 1876, William Wells, prominent Physician for St David's and Speaker of the House, had been the sole objector who expressed concerns when the vote was taken to petition the Queen to make Grenada a Crown Colony.

MOVING ON

During this period of disaffection, the majority of ordinary folk continued to conduct their simple lives by carrying out daily routines that were necessary for survival. Dee Dee was at that time mainly concerned with caring for her precious baby girl, even though there was no shortage of volunteers willing to look after the new arrival. Everyone appeared enamoured of the delightful and engaging child, who was being affectionately called 'Angie'.

On hearing the news that he had a second daughter, Simon felt an overwhelming desire to see her. He approached Sam while he was ploughing the land with an offer of apology and politely sought permission to visit the family home. Sam could hardly believe his ears. He had not forgotten Simon's disgraceful stance on being told that Dee Dee was with child and asked sarcastically if Simon had at long last found his 'manners'. But, after delivering a stern lecture, Sam consented to the younger man's request. Simon expressed humble and sincere appreciation and within hours had seen his baby daughter for the very first time. Little Angie would be the catalyst for the harmonious platonic relationship that eventually developed between her parents.

In 1884, Grenada was gripped by an epidemic of a deadly and contagious disease called Cholera. The people were advised to whitewash their houses and for the most part remain indoors. Cousin B, in particular, was fearful of the potential risks to the siblings in her care and having to give account for those whom she described as being 'other people's children'. She prayed diligently each day that they would be spared contamination. After two months the epidemic was over and 'by the Grace of God' no-one in the small community had been struck down with the feared illness. The people were greatly relieved and the women organised a prayer meeting to give thanks to the Almighty for escaping a visit from the dreaded disease.

Despite the responsibilities associated with being a single mother, Dee Dee was also expected to continue with the tasks she had been required to carry out prior to giving birth. Dee Dee looked forward to Sunday, which historically was the nation's day of rest. And afternoons were often spent visiting friends and relatives in the small village of Dudmar, where groups of young and old engaged in local gossip, while children played around them.

During those idle Sunday afternoons, Dee Dee became acquainted with a tall, brown-skinned man with a mop of curly hair, whose toddler son, Evan, had been little Angie's best play mate. As time went by, Dee Dee and Etienne found that they were comfortable in each other's company and a friendship developed between them. Even so, Dee Dee secretly questioned why this good-looking, eligible young bachelor, who was admired and sought after by the majority of unattached girls in the locality, would be interested in befriending her. The unlikely couple looked forward to their Sunday get-together and being with friends and relatives for the usual humorous banter and relaying of juicy gossip. And so it was, at the beginning of November 1885, Dee Dee, Etienne and others were reflecting on the recent All Saints and All Souls religious ceremonies when news broke that the annually held Guy Fawkes celebrations in St George's Town had been cancelled.

The ban was implemented under a new Law forbidding the lighting of bonfires or discharging of fireworks in the market square or any public place. The St George's community and the nation in general were profoundly angered and aggrieved. There was general consensus that this new Law was unjust and unwarranted. The nation was unable to fathom why the British would go to such lengths as to put a stop to their lively but peaceful expression of culture. Simmering national discontent that the people of the island had no voice reached boiling point. Anger fermented and rebellious action was put in train. Hand-written leaflets calling on citizens to 'stand up' for their rights were circulated in the town of St George. The people were resolute that one of the few privileges enjoyed under Crown Colony Government would not be withdrawn. On the night of 4th November 1885, ordinary people as well as individuals from the educated middle classes rose together in defiance of the newly passed Law. Bonfires were lit in the market place, tar barrels were ignited, street lamps were smashed and the town was plunged into darkness.

The nation was consolidated by the riots. The political injustices of the day were magnified and the people united in demanding a Government that would uphold and respect their opinions, culture, rights and privileges. The struggle for self-determination had been triggered and would continue for many decades.

It was with unprecedented anticipation that the population looked forward to the total eclipse of the sun predicted over the island in 1886. Grenadians had not in recent history experienced such an event and the day was saluted with bated breath. Several Astronomers lodged themselves on Green Island, a tiny uninhabited island in close proximity to Grenada, and with binoculars waited patiently to observe the once-in-a-lifetime phenomenon. But the weather was stubbornly uncompromising and the skies remained overcast throughout the day. Nothing of significance was seen by people in Grenada or the Astronomers on Green Island. Only those with telescopes on the sister island of Carriacou were successful in obtaining a clear view of the much-anticipated eclipse. It had been a hugely disappointing day for the people.

A DOOR OPENS

For Dee Dee and her family, 1886 was destined to be a significant year. Dee Dee had no idea that Etienne secretly admired her pretty smile and friendly manner and was exactly the kind of girl he desired as a life partner. She also had no clue that the eligible young bachelor had approached Pa Sam and asked for her hand in marriage. And that Sam, without hesitation, had given his consent. It had been a great compliment to Sam that a fine young gentleman like Etienne Lett considered Dee Dee worthy to be his wife. Grandma Millie and the rest of the family were equally delighted. Cousin B said it was a prime example of the 'Good Lord working in mysterious ways, his wonders to perform'. Simon had shut the door on Dee Dee but a bigger door was now being opened. Cousin B conceded that she may have been wrong in assuming that Dee Dee had no luck.

Dee Dee knew nothing of her own proposed marriage until it was announced by Sam, in the presence of Etienne, at a family gathering arranged for that very purpose. Dee Dee was stunned into silence. She had been completely unaware of Etienne's intentions and thought of him as no more than a good friend. It was indeed a mind-blowing surprise and Dee Dee could not help but pinch herself to make sure that she had not been dreaming. It was hard to conceive that the most sought-after young man in the community chose her above others to be his wife! After the disappointment and heartbreak of her association with Simon, Dee Dee was happy and relieved to have found herself a better man. She could barely wait to write and inform her mother, Hope, of the exciting news.

The marriage betrothal was soon common knowledge and the community buzzed with delight. The majority were genuinely pleased that Dee Dee had found herself a 'good man', after everything 'the poor girl' had been through. "God is good," they said. Meanwhile, Dee Dee and Etienne, whose relationship was based on friendship rather than passion, continued their Sunday afternoon sessions with relatives and friends in Dudmar. But Dee Dee was now somewhat shy and a little self-conscious whenever Etienne made eye contact with her.

Hope was over the moon when news reached her of Dee Dee's intended marriage to Etienne Lett. She embarked on an immediate shopping spree and despatched a parcel to her daughter. Among the contents were material for making the bridal gown and veil and a pair of fashionable white boots. Dee Dee was thrilled with her gift and the wedding preparations stepped up a gear when nominated relatives and friends got down to work in their separate roles. It included shopping for necessary items, baking the wedding cake, sewing the bridal gown and fattening a pig for the wedding feast.

The wedding day of Dee Dee and Etienne arrived; and family and friends, dressed in specially made outfits, set off on foot for the Church in St David's proper. Dee, in her fine bridal gown and veil, which fell over her face, clutched a posy of white lilies as she followed on the back of a lethargic and slow-trotting donkey. The journey may have been quicker on foot, but the risk of Dee Dee's shiny white boots being soiled by mud was too great. Pa Sam led the donkey and Grandma Millie and Cousin B shuffled alongside. It was the rainy season and, though the weather was mostly warm and sunny, they were not spared the occasional downpour.

Etienne, family members and invited guests were seated at the Church and awaiting the bridal party for some time when, dampened by rain, they finally arrived. Flanked by her father Sam, Grandma Millie and Cousin B, Dee Dee walked up the aisle and took her place beside the waiting groom. The ceremony began and the couple repeated their marriage vows in turn.

At the end of the Church ceremony, Dee Dee proudly walked down the aisle on the arm of her newly wedded husband and remounted the donkey that had been tied to a nearby tree. Etienne walked alongside, holding the rope that was secured around the animal's neck, and the entourage was led on an unhurried trek to Cousin B's yard, where the reception was being held. On arrival and after the customary lengthy and boring speeches, guests as well as gatecrashers were treated to stewed pork and chicken served with various provisions. Cake, sorrel and ginger beer were also served. There followed the inevitable singing, clapping and dancing to the rhythm of a solitary drum, and a jolly time was had by all.

When the celebrations were over, Angie was left in the temporary care of Cousin B while Etienne introduced his bride to the couple's newly built house in Dudmar.

The front door opened into the drawing room and Dee Dee's eyes were immediately drawn to a glass cabinet filled with beautiful tureens. She stood in awe and rubbed her eyes in disbelief. "Dar one look jes like de one Cousin B have," she exclaimed. Etienne smiled, placed a hand on his bride's shoulder and explained that the cabinet was a surprise gift from Cousin B. She had decided that the family heirloom should be passed on to Dee Dee, who had become the daughter she never had. Dee Dee could not help feeling overcome with emotion. It seemed unreal that this most admired piece of furniture, complete with contents, now belonged to her. Her childhood dream of being married, having a big house and a cabinet filled with china dishes and colourful glasses had been fulfilled, and all at the same time. Dee Dee felt that her heart would burst with happiness as it pounded forcefully against her chest. She clasped her hands together and, looking upward, cried, "Thank God. Thank you, Lord. Thank you."

The very next morning, following a night of bliss with her new husband, Dee Dee picked two of the best-looking mangoes from the tree and presented them to Cousin B in appreciation of her most generous gift.

MARRIED WITH A STEP-DAUGHTER

Dee Dee and Etienne settled contentedly into married life along with little Angie and after just nine months Dee Dee gave birth to the couple's first child. The infant girl was called Alfreda.

Similar to the majority of husbands of the age, Etienne expected that his new wife would at all times abide by the marriage vow of obedience. And when she was not looking

Dee Dee: Astute, strong-minded and magnanimous.

after the home and family, Dee Dee was required to work the land alongside her husband. Etienne was a hard-working and forward-looking man whose main goal in life was to purchase many acres of property for ensuring a secure future for his offspring. Dee Dee was supportive and shared her husband's aspirations for their growing family.

Dee Dee was focused on performing her duties as a wife and mother to the best of her abilities and family life ran smoothly until little Angie contracted an aggressive strain of yaws. Yaws was a contagious skin disease prevalent among children of the period. Dee Dee's desperate attempts to cure the condition with traditional remedies failed. The child was taken to the doctor, but the prescribed medicine had no effect and she was admitted to the General Hospital in St George's. The treatment Angie received included being taken each morning for a sea bath, followed by a whole body massage with large handfuls of salted butter. Her condition improved steadily and after four weeks Angie was well enough to be discharged into the care of her family. But Etienne was unhappy and decided that Angie should not return to the family home. He believed there was residual infection in the child's system and feared it could be contracted by his beloved Alfreda. It was in no uncertain terms that Etienne instructed Dee Dee to deliver Angie into the care of her biological father, Simon.

Despite being heartbroken about having to give up her precious daughter, Dee Dee was well aware of her place as a wife. Her husband's decision was final and must be obeyed. There could be no negotiation.

Simon did not object to having his daughter live with him and assured Dee Dee that, with help and support from family and friends, the child would be well looked after. Angie very much looked forward to being reunited with her mother after several weeks in hospital and was unable to understand why she was being placed with her father. Angie had not been given a reason for being no longer welcomed in the family home. She was consumed with feelings of sadness and confusion and was frequently tearful. Simon attempted to console his daughter with offers of food, but Angie refused to eat and remained distressingly homesick. At that same time, Dee Dee was engulfed in grief for her absent eldest daughter and worried continuously about the well-being of her child. At the end of the second week of separation, which to Dee Dee seemed more like two months, she suddenly discovered her inner strength and decided to end the mental torture by taking matters into her own hands. Risking the wrath of her husband, Dee Dee presented herself in Simon's yard and reclaimed her daughter. Angie was delighted and laughed and skipped all the way home.

It was not until mother and daughter arrived in the family yard that Dee Dee was suddenly struck with the reality of what she had done. She realised that she had acted in a moment of madness and may have committed a sin by breaking the vow of obedience. Nonetheless, Dee Dee was determined to hold on to her little girl and braced herself for Etienne's reaction.

As expected, Etienne's expression turned to one of anger when he arrived home to find Angie in the yard playing with her little sister, Alfreda. He was furious at having been so blatantly disobeyed by his wife and demanded answers. Dee Dee responded in a calm and measured manner. She knew that her husband was fundamentally a God-fearing man and decided to appeal to his better nature. She explained that Angie had been distressed, refusing food and heading for relapse, and Dee Dee felt that the couple would be 'punished by God' if anything bad should happen to the 'poor child'. Etienne had been stopped in his tracks, but was not prepared to lose face by openly conceding that Dee Dee may be right. The thought of offending God and possibly committing a mortal sin by sending away an innocent child, which may result in the return of her illness, was daunting for Etienne. But his manly sense of pride prevented any show of vulnerability and he chose to remain silent. Etienne's demeanour indicated to

Dee Dee that she had won the argument. Her husband had not suspected that a strong-minded and shrewd character lay beneath the meek persona of his wife and that she had cleverly used a ploy for overturning his command. Dee Dee could not help being secretly self-congratulatory. She offered a quiet prayer of thanksgiving and vowed that she would never again be parted from her beloved first daughter.

Life for the family continued as normal and nothing further was said regarding Angie's return to the fold. Dee Dee's mind was now at peace and it was not long before she was expecting again. But Etienne doted on his delightful little 'princess' Alfreda and often presented her with gifts such as tiny gold bangles purchased from Syrian tradesmen. Angie stared longingly at her sister's jewellery and wished that she also would be given a beautiful bangle. She made every effort to please her stepfather in the hope that her wish would one day be granted, but it was not to be. Favouring one child above the other was in those days never concealed or even frowned upon. Disparity in its various forms was generally considered a reality of life. Even so, Dee Dee was not too happy that Angie was being ignored by Etienne, but thanked God that she was back in her care. Dee Dee made sure that Angie was compensated by providing her with plenty of her favourite food.

The family expanded over the years and between them Etienne and Dee Dee produced a total of eight children, who called their parents Dee Dee and Pa Way.

As Angie grew older, she was charged with looking after her younger brothers and sisters when Dee Dee worked the land alongside Pa Way. But she regularly left the children unattended to go craw fishing in a stream at the bottom of the yard with her best friend Matty. The girls always kept an ear open for Pa Way and Dee Dee's footsteps as they returned home. And at that point Angie would sprint back to the house, sit on a chair and place the youngest child on her lap. The couple were reassured that all was well when they returned to find Angie sitting by the door holding the baby and being surrounded by the older children. Dee Dee would immediately begin preparing dinner and when it was ready, Angie was given a dish of the freshly cooked meal to take to Dee Dee's best friend, Mrs Brizanne, who coincidentally was the mother of Angie's own best friend, Matty.

Angie felt it an injustice that she should have to carry out the errand before being permitted to eat her share of the meal and while the rest of the family were tucking into theirs. She would console herself by seeking out and popping into her mouth the largest piece of meat or fish on the plate, before delivering the dish in a demure fashion that never failed to impress upon the recipient that she was indeed an innocent, sweet natured and well mannered young girl.

Despite the perceived injustices, Angie remained close to her mother and enjoyed their exclusive time together. Mother and daughter prepared produce for selling at market and walked side by side en route to Grenville with tightly packed baskets perched on their heads. They were on occasions accompanied by Pa Way with a loaded donkey. On arrival, the family would select a prime spot, where their various products were displayed for sale. At the end of the market day, Dee Dee and Angie would use a percentage of the profits to purchase necessary items such as boxes of matches, kerosene for fuelling lamps or lanterns, blocks of soap, salt, flour and fresh or salted meat and fish.

Tradition dictated that every Sunday the family dressed in their best outfits and joined with others for the long walk to and from Church through rugged terrain. Dee Dee and Pa Way's children were among the privileged who owned shoes that were permitted to be worn only on Sundays or special occasions. It was not, in those days, uncommon for individuals to carry their shoes or boots over their shoulder during the hazardous journey and put them on just prior to entering Church. Many who tripped and severely injured a foot would make a Sign of the Cross and thank God that they had not been wearing their shoes. Damaging treasured footwear was in those days far more distressing than the sharp and intense pain that resulted from stumping a toe or more.

As in previous generations, everyone expected to be treated to a special breakfast when they returned to their separate homes at the end of the Service. Dee Dee's family received large portions of a fry-up, which usually included fried bake, fish cakes and eggs, served with a side salad consisting of avocado, cucumber and tomatoes.

Dee Dee' parenting style was modelled on the way she was raised by Cousin B. Dee Dee was, by nature, a warm-hearted and generous woman. She strived to be a caring and compassionate mother and physical chastisement was rarely used on the siblings. But in line with tradition, the children were required to carry out routine chores and were only sent to school if and when the work was completed.

Despite the demands of family life, Dee Dee remained a classy and smartly dressed woman. She maintained a relatively beautiful home, which contained the finest mahogany furniture and her treasured glass cabinet occupied pride of place.

Pa Way was an intelligent man from a good family background. He chose Dee Dee as his life partner because of her elegance, friendly manner and bright smile. Importantly for Pa Way, Dee Dee was a humble-natured and compliant woman. Despite the difficulties relating to Angie, Pa Way was not disappointed with his choice of woman. Dee Dee worked 'like any man' on the land, prepared tasty meals, looked after house and family and was an amorous bed mate. "What more could any husband wish for?" he asked himself.

There were those in the community who coveted the couple's comparative wealth; young women were particularly resentful of Dee Dee, and were unable to understand how she was able to catch such a fine husband. They had no idea that even the envied wife was similarly mystified. The women begrudged the way Dee Dee paraded in her stylish frocks, matching turbans, gold beads, bangles and laced boots. They considered her no more than a 'show off' and their resentment spilled over when they decided that the time had come to teach 'Madam Lett' a lesson. Dee Dee was waylaid and surrounded by her enemies as she returned home one day. She was punched and shoved around, before being knocked to the ground, kicked and spat upon. After their venom was fully spewed, the assailants fled, leaving the victim bruised and traumatised. Dee Dee picked herself up and limped to the nearest river, where she cleaned herself up and brushed down her bodice and gathered up her skirt before making her way home.

Dee Dee did not mention the incident to anyone, but her inherent sense of worth and steely underlying character were in no way dented. She maintained her stylish stance, continued to dress elegantly, held her head high and considered herself a cut above the rest.

ANGIE

Angie grew up in the knowledge that Simon Telesford was her biological father. Father and daughter were in regular contact and related well with each other. Despite being treated less favourably than the other children by Pa Way, Angie was happy to remain in the care of her mother, with whom she was closely bonded and felt secure. Angie also shared caring relationships with Grandpa Sam, Grandma Millie, Cousin B and the rest of the extended family. She maintained close pals with her stepbrother, Evan. The pair had been playmates as toddlers and remained close for the rest of their lives.

Angie attended school only on days when she was not required to be at home to look after her younger siblings. She was a bright girl, or, as Dee Dee would say, 'her head dor hard', which meant that she was naturally intelligent. Though her schooling was sporadic, Angie managed to grasp the basic principles of reading and writing before her school career was terminated when she was just 13 years of age. She was at that point sent to Miss Ada Purcell, a reputable seamstress in the community, to be taught skills in dressmaking and embroidery. Nearly every young girl on the island at the time was expected to be skilled in sewing, cooking, baking and other homemaking requirements, in preparation for being a wife and mother, and they took precedence over academia.

Angie was still only 13 years of age when Dee Dee gave birth to her youngest daughter, Evie. The infant was born prematurely and not expected to survive for more than a few hours. The priest was called and the newborn was baptised. Angie, being the oldest of the young females in the house at the time, was called upon to be godmother.

In spite of the grim prognosis, Dee Dee refused to give up hope and maintained faith. When she was not attempting to feed her baby from the breast, Dee Dee would hold the infant closely and firmly, as if to breathe life into her fragile little body. She prayed that God would spare the life of her child and was joined in prayer by family and friends who gathered at the house. After a long and uncertain night, the morning was greeted with relief. Evie had miraculously survived the critical hours. Everyone present dropped to their knees and thanked God that their prayers had been answered. It proved a significant turning point, as from that day onwards Evie strived and steadily gained weight.

Angie was charged with looking after baby Evie on a regular basis. She became the child's 'little mother' and an attachment developed between them. As she grew into a toddler, Evie began referring to Angie as 'Nen'. The older siblings followed suit and Angie eventually became known as 'Nen' among family members and friends. It was a term that would be passed down the generations.

The years evaporated and in time the nation joined the rest of the world by bidding farewell to the old century and welcoming the new. Angie was 16 years old in 1900 and excitedly looking forward to being a bridesmaid for the very first time at the marriage between her best friend Matty and one Albert Redhead. Angie was particularly hoping to get together with Albert's younger brother George, on whom she had a secret crush. Angie often day-dreamed about having a romantic association with George and would lie in bed at night thinking about him. She was enamoured of his tall, lean physique and smoothly brushed shiny hair. Angie's heart skipped a beat and her stomach flipped whenever she caught sight of George and pictured herself walking down the aisle with him.

The day of the wedding arrived and, dressed in her specially designed outfit, Angie walked down the aisle at the Parish Church, behind the bride with other similarly dressed bridesmaids. She was delighted to be a first-time bridesmaid, but her mind was focused on George. She hoped he would find her attractive in her pretty new dress. But it was not to be. Angie struggled to keep her eyes off George, as he looked so handsome, but George showed no interest in Angie. He ignored her throughout the church ceremony and at the reception that followed. Angie concealed her disappointment and tried to appear cheerful as she mingled with other young people at the gathering. But she was heartbroken and her night was spent sobbing silently into her pillow. Angie decided to reveal the secret love she harboured for George to Matty when they met up a few weeks after the wedding, but was dismayed to be told by her best friend, who was now George's new sister-in-law, that her heart's desire would never consider befriending a girl as young as Angie and preferred girls who were nearer his own age. The realisation that she might never get the boy of her dreams was a crushing disappointment for Angie. She was mystified that George, who, at age 20, was just four years her senior, should consider her too young for him. Angie had a sinking feeling that she had no choice but to accept the fact that she was just not pretty enough for handsome George.

CATCHING UP

In the year 1892, William Radix, who lived in the village of Boca, celebrated his 16th birthday. He was at that time holding a teaching position at the Parish school and was also a talented cricketer who played in inter-parish matches up and down the island.

William was 24 years old in the year 1900. He was at that stage a popular and respected young man in his locality. He had resigned from his teaching post after deciding to go into business and now owned a general store. William no longer played cricket, but acted as umpire at organised matches throughout the island. Tant Cecae worried that, at 24 years of age, her son was still single and reluctant to be serious with any of the girls he befriended. Even though William loved being in the company of young women, he was happy living a free and single life. He enjoyed socialising with other single men and had no intention of marrying until the right person came along. William was stubbornly not prepared to settle for second best.

BOY MEETS GIRL

Two months after experiencing the pain of being rejected by her first love interest, Angie and a group of friends one Sunday afternoon went to see a cricket match being played at the ball field in the village of Vincennes. It was the day that Angie was destined to meet her fate.

Angie was totally unaware of the moment she was spotted by the umpire. William Radix had momentarily cast his eyes across the spectators and was drawn to a pretty young girl standing among the crowd. He knew instinctively that she was the woman he would marry. He stole glimpses of her at every opportune moment and at the end of the match enquired into the background of the young lady of interest from one of the local players. William was told that her name was Angie Telesford. She was single, had no children, was able to read and write and that her family owned 'plenty land'.

It seemed to William that this girl had ticked all the boxes. Not only was she beautiful, but also intelligent, and came from a good family. William made a decision.

The following Sunday afternoon, a smartly dressed William arrived in the Lett's yard on horseback. Dee Dee and Pa Way, who had been sitting quietly and contentedly smoking their pipe while the children were pursuing separate interests, were surprised by the unexpected appearance of this well-groomed, striking-looking young stranger and looked at each other with puzzled expressions. William walked towards the couple after dismounting from his horse, introduced himself and politely asked to speak to them. He was led into the drawing room, offered a seat on the cushioned mahogany sofa and Dee Dee served him with a plate of food and a glass of ginger beer.

William maintained his composure and, with eyes fixed on Pa Way , gave a brief account of his background before disclosing his interest in Angie. Dee Dee and Pa Way listened intently as the young man spoke and were intrigued by his unusual accent. Suddenly, William was asking for their daughter's hand in marriage and the couple were astounded and rendered speechless. On regaining their equanimity, Pa Way was the first to speak by revealing that he had no idea that William even knew his daughter. William explained that, although he had seen Angie and enquired into her background, the pair had not yet been introduced to each other.

On hearing William's honourable intentions, Dee Dee broke into a huge smile. She was instantly delighted that such a fine, well-spoken and respectful-looking young man who rode a horse was interested in her daughter. Pa Way displayed no outward emotion, but was quietly sceptical of the young 'foreigner'. He nonetheless remained calm and polite, while explaining to William that his proposal would be considered and that he should return to the house two weeks to the day for a definitive answer to his request. Dee Dee made sure that William was refreshed with a repeat of a large cool drink before setting off on his return journey home.

Following William's departure, Dee Dee and Pa Way reflected on their shock and amazement by the 'out of the blue' proposal of marriage from a complete stranger. It seemed unbelievable. Pa Way expressed mistrust of 'foreigners', a reason for which he was totally against the match. But Dee Dee decided against revealing that her maternal instinct suggested that William would be perfect for her daughter. She was well aware that her words must be carefully chosen before attempting to challenge her husband's decision. On being told of William's unexpected appearance and subsequent proposal, Sam and Simon also voiced shared concerns. There was an unspoken rule that unions with individuals of the opposite sex who resided beyond the boundaries of their community should not be encouraged, and that a relationship formed between relatives would be the preferred option.

Dee Dee was in a dilemma. Her loyalties were torn between being obedient to her husband and following her maternal intuition. As far as Dee Dee was concerned, William was a young man with 'prospects' and exactly what she would wish for young Angie. She had a gut feeling that William would be a good husband and decided to put forward her case calmly but firmly. Dee Dee explained that she understood the men's fears, but pointed out that William was a man of respectable standing and should provide 'well' for their girl. She then presented her trump card by suggesting that a supervisory eye could be kept on William if he lived locally. After some deliberation, the men came to the conclusion that Dee Dee's proposal could be accepted if William did indeed agree to relocate into their community. Dee Dee was filled with a quiet sense of victorious satisfaction. She had once again won the day on an issue that was important and dear to her heart. Her diplomatic approach and iron-fisted velvet-gloved methods never failed.

When Dee Dee sat Angie down and told her about William's unexpected visit, his expressed interest and proposal of marriage, Angie was amazed and bewildered. She could not understand why a complete stranger would ask for her hand in marriage. It seemed that one minute she was heartbroken, feeling forlorn and wondering if any boy would ever find her attractive; and the next minute she was being told that she would very likely be getting married. Unbelievable, she thought. Suddenly, Angie's mind switched to the suitor's possible appearance. Similar to a majority of young females, looks were of primary importance and she was fearful that the prospective suitor might be 'ugly'. Why else would he want to marry a plain-looking girl like herself, she reasoned. But marrying an ugly young man was an unbearable prospect for Angie.

The following two weeks were filled with stomach-churning mixed feelings of anxiety, fear, curiosity and apprehension and sleepless nights. The days leading to William's second visit to the family home, in Angie's view, dragged slowly as she tried to make sense of the significant life-changing events about to unfold that were completely beyond her control. She was very much aware that as a minor she had no right of say in the matter and would be obliged to abide by the wishes of her parents.

Angie was edgy, restless and felt physically sick on the day of William's scheduled visit. Close family members joined together in the yard dressed in their Sunday best and waited with expectancy for the young man's arrival. Angie sat a little distance away under the shade of a tree, unable to calm the involuntary twitching of her legs. Suddenly, the group was alerted by the clattering hooves of an approaching horse and within a few short minutes William was standing in the yard with a buxom woman of light complexion by his side. Everyone present surrounded the guests and extended a welcoming hand. William introduced the woman as his mother, Tant Cecae, and the party moved into the house. Dee Dee served up large portions of food on her best china, followed by tropical juice in patterned glasses. It had been one of the very few occasions that Dee Dee brought out her treasured chinaware and indicated the importance of the occasion.

After the meal and some general small talk, Pa Way acted as spokesperson and informed William of the family's decision. If William agreed to the stipulated condition, he would be permitted to visit Angie every Sunday afternoon prior to the wedding. William was overjoyed and pledged compliance, but would no doubt have pledged agreement to any term or condition that had been placed before him. It was from the bottom of his heart that William thanked the family for accepting his proposal to marry their beautiful daughter.

Everyone present hugged each other or shook hands after the proposal of marriage was orally endorsed by all present. Dee Dee poured ginger beer into flower-patterned glasses and a toast was raised to the coming together of the two families. Tant Cecae laughed heartily as she threw her hefty arms around each family member in turn, exclaiming exuberantly, "All yuh is we new famarly! Arr soo glad. Arr soo glad. Arr too happy!" She thanked God that her precious boy had at long last found himself a wife.

All the while, an out-of-sight Angie sat nervously waiting to be summoned before her elders. She could hear raised voices and laughter coming from the house and wondered what was going on. She had caught a glimpse of William as he arrived on horseback and at that point vaguely recalled that he had umpired the cricket match she attended with friends a few weeks previously. Angie could not understand why, of all the girls at the match that day, she was singled out by William, but was very much relieved that her fear that he would be an unattractive young man had been unfounded.

Angie did not consider herself particularly pretty, even though various individuals had from to time commented on her 'nice complexion'. Angie had a fascination with hair, but disliked her own, which was short and brittle, and she wished for long shiny plaits like her beautiful younger sisters.

Angie was jolted out of her thoughts and was quickly on her feet when she realised that the party had left the house and was walking towards her. Suddenly, Dee Dee's hand was on Angie's arm and she was being guided towards William. "Come and meet de nice man yuh gonna marry," her mother said. Dee Dee introduced the couple to each other. William extended a hand and told Angie he was 'pleased' to meet her. Angie mumbled nervously in similar vein. At that point, Tant Cecae stepped forward and, with full force, threw herself at Angie, almost knocking backwards the slightly built frame of the young girl with her large and extended breasts. She cupped Angie's cheeks between her palms and shrieked with happiness that her son had found himself such a pretty wife and from a good family too. Angie could not help being flattered to be told that she was pretty. She had never before been so highly complimented and was immediately charmed by the mother-in-law-to- be.

William, Tant Cecae and the rest of the family returned to the house to continue their discussion while Angie remained in the yard. She was now desperately trying to get her head around the reality of the situation. She was just 16 years old and still only a child. The idea that she would soon be someone's wife was a daunting prospect. "Oh my God," she prayed. "Please help me." But Angie knew that Dee Dee would not have agreed to the marriage if she did not feel it was right and reassured herself that her mother was at all times protective of her best interests. Angie's thoughts then switched to William. She had briefly assessed his appearance as they shook hands and was satisfied that he was indeed a good-looking young man. She particularly liked William's neatly combed wavy hair, but her eyes lingered for a moment or two on his large nose. Angie had not previously seen one so big and was unable to control the giggles as she recalled the up-close viewing.

Angie came to the conclusion that, overall, William was really quite a handsome young gentleman. He was of average build and height, dressed well and spoke like their parish priest, commonly known as 'Father'. To crown it all, William rode a horse and that was quite something in those days for one so young. Apart from George Redhead, Angie could think of no better suitor than William Radix.

Soon, William and Tant Cecae were bidding goodbye and mounting their horses for the return journey to the Black Forest. Both were satisfied that their visit to the prospective in-laws had been worthwhile and productive. The desired result had been achieved, despite the compromise of William being required to leave the village of his birth and start afresh in the parish of St David's.

News of Angie's engagement to William spread across the community and became a hot topic of conversation and debate. Many people were outraged that Dee Dee and Pa Way had broken the unwritten code by consenting to their daughter marrying a 'foreigner'. Only a minority of people in the community supported the union and opinions were openly expressed and discussed.

THE COURTSHIP

The days leading to William's first visit following the betrothal had been a nail-bitingly anxious time for Angie. She wondered whether they would be allowed to be alone together and, if so, what would she say to him, or vice versa. Angie was filled with trepidation. The due day finally arrived and the family sat in the yard and waited. Dee Dee, who had been happily looking forward to seeing William again, was unable to conceal her delight when he eventually appeared. She greeted him warmly and William shook the hand of Pa Way before nodding politely to Angie. Dee Dee invited William into the house, where he was served the customary generous portion of a cooked meal followed by a large cool drink. After the meal was eaten, Angie was encouraged by her parents to join William in the drawing room. Pa Way and Dee Dee remained in the yard and contentedly smoked their pipes. It was an era when pipe smoking was common-place with both men and women.

While they were alone together, Angie discovered that her fears may have been misplaced. She was quickly put at ease by William when he tenderly held both of her hands and expressed his feelings in heartfelt and soft-spoken words. But the couple's first meeting had been short and before too long William was remounting his horse and heading for home. That night, Angie lay awake in her bed on the floor and tingled with excitement as romantic thoughts of William washed over her. It had been her very first experience of being alone with a boy, but the 'click' between the couple had been almost immediate. Angie would find herself counting down the days to William's next visit.

William kept to the schedule laid down by Dee Dee and Pa Way and visited Angie every Sunday afternoon. The couple regularly engaged in activities such as socialising with friends, fishing or simply going for long walks. Angie was always a supportive spectator whenever William played cricket with other young men in the vicinity. But private tender moments were inevitably snatched in cleared areas within the dense plantation when they abandoned themselves to charged emotions and Angie could do nothing but succumb to William's amorous embraces. One of their most memorable and enjoyable moments was the occasion they accompanied each other to a dance event. The couple held each other close as they blissfully danced the night away. But the magical interlude would not be repeated. It was the one and only ball the couple attended together.

THE WEDDING PLANNING

While Angie and William were steadily building a close and loving relationship during several months of courtship, Dee Dee was busy with the meticulous planning of the wedding of her eldest daughter. She was focused on making it the most spectacular event of 1901 in the parish of St David's.

The first item on Dee Dee's agenda was a shopping expedition to Trinidad and she wrote a letter to Hope telling her all about Angie's engagement and the planned trip.

Not long afterwards, Dee Dee set off on her journey across the seas while the younger children remained in the care of Angie and Pa Way. Eighteen years had passed since Dee Dee last visited her mother and sister and she was anxious to see them again. But, on boarding the vessel, Dee Dee was reminded of the grim experience of her first boat journey back in 1883 and was suddenly gripped with feelings of apprehension. She prayed that this trip would be less harrowing. When the vessel finally pulled in at the pier in Port of Spain, Dee Dee offered a prayer of thanksgiving. The journey, in comparison, had been fairly comfortable. Hope and May were waiting to welcome Dee Dee on her arrival and she was greeted with open arms. May, who was just eight years old when Dee Dee last saw her, had grown into an attractive young woman and was married with a seven-year-old daughter. And here was Dee Dee,, about to embark on a shopping trip for the wedding of the daughter she did not even know she was expecting when she last visited her mother and sister.

A few days after the euphoria of the reunion, Dee Dee, accompanied by Hope, embarked on the much-anticipated shopping spree. Dee Dee was once again captivated by the comparative vibrancy of Port of Spain and the various retail outlets. She was spoilt for choice, but her eventual purchases included 24 yards of cashmere silk and lace for making the bridal gown, veil material, white satin slippers and a set of pearls with matching earrings.

Dee Dee begged Hope to accompany her on the return journey to Grenada. She very much desired her mother's involvement in the wedding planning and in particular her presence at the ceremony. Hope was delighted that her grand-daughter would be marrying a fine and upstanding young gentleman, as Dee Dee described William to be. She would have loved to accept her daughter's invitation, but feared jeopardising her much-guarded and cherished hard-earned freedom and independence.

After returning home, Dee Dee commissioned Mrs Sweeney, a skilled seamstress of high regard, to design and stitch the bridal ensemble. A carriage drawn by white horses with plumage was hired for transporting the bride and groom. Separate horses and riding habits were ordered for the bridesmaids. Dee Dee, who had been taken to her own wedding on the back of a slow-trotting, lethargic donkey, desired pomp and style for her daughter.

During the period that Dee Dee and various members of the extended family were occupied with preparing for the forthcoming nuptials and the community buzzed in anticipation, no-one could have foreseen the tragic events that were about to unfold.

On 1st November 1900, the SS *Orinoco*, a ship en route to St George's harbour, was wrecked. The Captain mistook the numerous candles that had been lit in memory of the deceased for those of the city and the ship was steered onto rocks along La Sagesse. A large number of passengers and crew perished when they were flung into the sea as the damaged vessel capsized and subsequently sank into the waters. The catastrophe sent shockwaves throughout the nation.

Despite the trauma caused by the disaster that occurred on their shores, Dee Dee did not feel that it was a totally valid reason for cancelling the wedding. Nothing could be changed and so much had already been done. It was Dee Dee's view also that altering the date of the marriage may have obstructed the smooth process of the wedding planning.

THE WEDDING

After much planning and preparation, everything was perfectly in place when the eagerly awaited wedding day of Angie and William finally arrived. The year was 1901. The bride was dressed in an embroidered flowing silk gown with extended train. White satin slippers peeped beneath the hemline. A delicately fine veil, secured with a crown of white roses, fell over her face. The ensemble was accessorised with a string of pearls and matching earrings. The bouquet consisted of red and white roses entwined in fern.

Angie, with Dee Dee elegantly dressed in a shiny sky-blue outfit sitting beside her, was taken from the family home to the Church in St David's proper in a carriage drawn by white horses with plumages of white feathers standing tall on their heads. The reins were held by a gentleman dressed in jacket and tie. Six bridesmaids in riding habits and on separate horses followed the carriage.

The father of the bride, Simon Telesford, rode ahead of the entourage, swinging a large bell signalling the oncoming bridal procession. Onlookers lined the route to the Church and clapped and cheered excitedly.

On entering the Church, the bride walked slowly up the aisle on the arm of her father, with the extended train attractively placed behind her. The bridesmaids and close family members followed. The organ began to play and waiting guests stood and in unison belted out the selected hymn.

William, who wore a newly tailored light-grey suit, gleaming white shirt and bow-tie, waited nervously with his brothers at the altar. As Angie arrived beside him, Dee Dee lifted the veil from her face and passed the bouquet to Angie's best friend Matty, who was the bridesmaid-in-chief. The couple's eyes met and they smiled. William was struck by the beauty of his bride and she had not seen him look more handsome.

After Angie and William had taken their vows and the marriage service was over, the happy couple and their entourage began the journey to the reception in Dudmar. It was a sunny and pleasant Sunday afternoon, but the sleepy environment was awakened by the clattering of horses' hooves, chiming bells, blowing whistles and a loudly cheering small crowd. Onlookers were overawed. They had never before seen so many horses and well-dressed riders at any one time in their community. Female guests were dressed in colourful dresses with matching turbans. The men wore white shirts and neck ties.

The newly married couple smiled as they sat beside each other in their open carriage. Individuals jostled to shake their hands, wish them luck or compliment their beautiful attire. There were those who followed the wedding cortege all the way to the village of Dudmar with the intention of participating in the wedding feast.

On arrival at the reception, the newly wedded couple were toasted with glasses of red wine. One of the guests was Angie's first love, George Redhead. George congratulated Angie, whose heart now belonged to William, by planting a moist kiss on her cheek. The elders delivered boring and seemingly endless speeches. Some predicted marital difficulties ahead and offered advice from personal experiences. Others told humorous stories regarding the couple's conduct prior to their marriage. Beaming with happiness, Tant Cecae, in gold attire, could hardly contain her joy as she stepped forward and announced proudly that she was the mother of the groom and was delighted he had given her such a beautiful daughter-in-law. After the speeches were over, the by then ravenous guests were served turtle soup followed by stewed chicken and pork with ground provision, okra, callaloo and stewed peas. Bread rolls, coconut buns, ginger beer, sorrel and tropical juice were readily available. The highlight was the cutting of the wedding cake. There was simultaneous clapping and cheering as the couple kissed after sharing by mouth a small portion of the cut cake. Then Dee Dee signalled to the waiting band and the music played for the couple's first dance. More clapping and cheering followed before everyone sprung to their feet in party mood as the music played on. The marriage of Angie and William had been wonderfully unforgettable, and Dee Dee was credited with 'pulling off' the most spectacular event of 1901 in the parish of St David's. Tant Cecae was particularly complimentary and praised Dee Dee for her extraordinary organisational skills. Although exhausted, Dee Dee was exhilarated. Her goal had been accomplished.

STARTING OUT

Angie and William needed helping hands to carry their many gifts to the marital home at the end of the reception. Wedding gifts included sets of bed-linen, bath towels, mortar and pestle, pots, pans and dishes. The bride received a matching basin and chamber pot from her mother, and maintained exclusive use of these practical essentials every day for the rest of her life.

The newly married couple began their life together in a tiny house in Dudmar. After a relatively short period, William opened up a small shop at the front of the premises where dried goods such as flour, crackers, salted meats and fish, tobacco and liquor could be purchased.

William was keen to build friendly relationships with customers and others in the locality, but many remained wary of his presence. Not only was William an outsider, it was compounded by the fact that he spoke and dressed differently from the majority and they felt unable to identify with him.

Angie could find no problem with her husband. She loved him dearly and the couple shared an intensely loving relationship. After a day of housekeeping routines and gardening, Angie looked forward to cosy evenings eating dinner with William and the passionate nights that followed. Within weeks of tying the knot, Angie found herself pregnant with the couple's first child. Ivan was born in January 1902. Angie, who was just 18 years of age, developed an immediate special bond with her beautiful first-born son.

William was not the stereotypical husband of the day and may have been ahead of his time. He loved and respected his wife and made an effort to maintain communication with her. It was his conscious decision that he would not be a cold and aloof husband and parent, as he remembered his own father to be. Despite being just seven years old when Papee passed away, William could not recall being engaged in dialogue with his father and regretted not having a parental relationship with him. Dee Dee's initial maternal intuition that William was the right man for her daughter was destined to be proven right.

Despite initial misgivings, William was gradually being accepted by a section of the community. He became well known for his academic capabilities and was frequently called upon by individuals to reply to letters, fill in forms or bear witness to and countersign documents such as written Wills.

The family business was doing reasonably well and William's shop became a popular meeting place, where young and old men congregated to buy and drink rum, play cards or simply socialise. The men invariably engaged in heated drunken arguments and there was never any compromising on trivial issues such as which variety of mango was the sweetest, whose wife made the tastiest sweet potato pudding or who could drink the most rum.

But there were those who begrudged the fact that 'the foreigner' (a name often used to describe William) had come into their community and was suddenly making more money than they were. Driven by bitter jealousy, they reported to the Authorities that William had been selling liquor without a licence.

William was alerted by a close friend and member of the local Council that a police raid on his shop was imminent. William panicked and hurriedly poured all the rum in his possession into the river, smashed the empty bottles and, without notifying anyone, fled the island. The year was 1903 and Angie was heavily into her second pregnancy.

WHERE IS WILLIAM?

Angie was distraught and mystified by her husband's sudden and unexplained absence and could neither eat nor sleep with worry. William was missing and could not be found, but rumours abounded that he had absconded because his shop was about to be busted. The community was in shock. Memories were refreshed of Hope's disappearance 28 years previously and older people recalled the sensational events. Dee Dee, who was so personally affected when her mother vanished into thin air, prayed that history was not being repeated.

Dee Dee was aware that her daughter was broken by William's unannounced departure and as a consequence was struggling to cope. She supported Angie by visiting her each day with a cooked meal and endeavoured to coax her into eating tiny portions. Food was in those days often used for providing comfort to those who were distressed or in some form of crisis. Tant Cecae was alarmed to learn of her son's disappearance, but did not believe he would abandon his young family without good reason. She attempted to assure Angie that William would return home some day soon, but Angie remained confused and unsure about the future of her marriage. The 'not knowing' was agonising, but Angie found solace from holding on tightly to her precious little son, Ivan. He was, in her view, a miniature version of his missing father.

During one of Dee Dee's daily visits, Angie began complaining of stomach pains, which quickly increased in frequency and severity. Dee Dee knew instinctively that her daughter was in premature labour, triggered possibly by the trauma of William's unexplained absence. Within a few short hours, Angie was on the floor and pushing into the world two babies, one after the other.

The women were pleasantly surprised. They had no idea that Angie had been expecting twins, but the arrival of the babies exacerbated Angie's feelings of aloneness and abandonment. She was now a 19-year-old mother of three and agonised about having the capacity to cope without the support of her husband.

Not long after the arrival of the twins, Dee Dee received a visit from an individual who said that his name was Manny. Manny alleged that he had encountered William on a vessel bound for Trinidad. William was tearful and disclosed that he was saddened that, due to unforeseen unfortunate circumstances, he had been forced to leave his 'wonderful' young wife and son, particularly at a time when she was carrying their second child. Manny's revelation left no doubt in Dee Dee's mind that the person on the boat was indeed William and wasted no time in conveying the heartening news to her daughter.

Angie was happily relieved to hear of Manny's encounter with William. It gave her hope that he was alive and well, wherever he was. Angie thanked God, but wished that William would at least write and let her know that he was safe. She found the uncertainty of it all most difficult, but prayed every day for her husband's safe return. Angie was now feeling less depressed and better able to cope with family commitments. But there was no shortage of offers of assistance from relatives and friends within the close-knit and supportive community. Then suddenly, out of the blue, Angie received notification that a letter had arrived at the Post Office and without hesitation it was collected by Dee Dee. Angie was curious but apprehensive as she carefully opened the envelope with trembling hands. She scanned her eyes across the page and quickly realised the letter had been written by William. She screamed with delight before reading the contents. The letter began with an apology. William stated he missed his 'darling wife' and promised to be home in the not-too-distant future. Angie was ecstatic. She made a sign of the cross with the letter clutched in her right hand and thanked God for answering her prayers, before throwing her arms around her mother, who had been standing beside her. Dee Dee was also happily relieved, and uttered her own quiet prayer of thanksgiving.

Soon Angie was putting pen to paper, telling her husband of the joy she felt on receiving his letter. She informed him of the birth of the couple's twins and how Ivan had grown into an inquisitive and boisterous toddler. Angie ended her letter by expressing the hope that it would not be long before William was reunited with the family.

William may have assumed that Angie had given birth to twin girls, but in his reply letter he suggested that the babies be named Clarice and Iris. Angie decided to honour William's request by naming the little girl Clarice and the boy Iris. Meanwhile, she continued to pray for her husband's safe return.

Tant Cecae, who visited her daughter-in-law on a fairly regular basis, was not surprised to hear that William had made contact, and exuded an air of triumph as she reminded Angie of her prediction that William would never abandon his family. Although appreciative of her mother-in-law's regular visits, Angie was wary of her criticism. Tant Cecae never failed to make disparaging remarks about the chaotic condition of the house and didn't take into account the difficulties involved with managing three very young, demanding children. Dee Dee, on the other hand, ignored the mess, but ensured that her own children assisted their big sister with routine outdoor chores. She also provided the family with a basket of groceries at the end of each week.

Ivan was at the time an active and boisterous toddler. He was always excited when his young aunts and uncles arrived on their daily visits. He enjoyed being chased, caught and tickled into fits of uncontrollable giggles. When the games were over, Ivan would follow the youngsters around the yard and stand beside them as they carried out their separate tasks.

WILLIAM RETURNS

Angie's prayers were fully answered when, out of the blue, William appeared in the yard. It was January 1904, ten months after his unexpected disappearance. On seeing her husband, Angie fell to her knees in shock and burst into tears of joy and relief. William lifted his wife onto her feet and the couple's embrace was lengthy and heartfelt. Angie was overwhelmed with happiness. Over and over again, she thanked God for her husband's safe return.

Little Ivan looked up at his parents curiously. He was unable to understand the moment and had no idea who the man was, but sensed the couple's happiness. Soon he would find himself being picked up and hugged by the large man with the smiling face. Ivan had been just 13 months old when William left the island, but was instantly comfortable in his father's arms. William was moved to tears when he saw his adorable twins Clarice and Iris for the very first time. He felt a calming sense of peace to be back where he belonged with his loving wife and beautiful children and considered himself truly blessed.

Breaking news of William's return was quickly picked up and the majority were genuinely happy that 'the poor girl's' husband, despite being a 'foreigner', was back home.

During the period spent abroad, William visited various countries in the region, such as Guyana and Barbados, seeking ideas for starting a new business, and he identified a gap in the market for cocoa and spices. He also discovered that cola nuts were among ingredients used for making Coca Cola, the popular new American fizzy beverage, being locally produced at a factory on the island of Trinidad.

After carrying out his research, William decided on an enterprise in export and import. He discussed his vision of a new business venture with Angie after returning home and she did not hesitate to give him her full support. But William's funds were limited and he needed land on which specific crop could be produced. Angie had an idea. She suggested that Pa Way should be approached for a loan. The Letts were known to be relatively prosperous, having vastly increased their ownership of land over the years.

William visited his father-in-law, cap in hand, and explained his business vision before requesting the required loan. It was refused. Instead, William was offered the loan of a specific piece of land which could be freely used for his business purposes. William was unable to think of a better outcome and his gratitude spilled over. He sprung to his feet, shook Pa Way's hand firmly and vigorously, and almost strangled his mother-in-law with the tightest of hugs.

William hurried home to Angie with the amazing news and she screamed, clapped and hugged her husband with delight. Pa Way's generosity was the opening of a pathway to future success.

William immediately got to work on his newly acquired land, but the family continued to struggle and were very much reliant on the weekly basket of groceries being provided by Dee Dee.

Not long after William's return, Angie found herself pregnant for the third time in as many years. She gave birth to a baby boy named John in November 1904.

The couple's difficulties seemed never ending and Angie decided that the time had come to do something to supplement the family's meagre income. Always a lover of gardening, she planted a variety of fruit and vegetables and, when the crop was ready, left the children in the care of her mother and took the produce to market, where they were sold for profit. William was dismayed that his wife should have to work to supplement the family's income. He considered himself a responsible husband and father who had been toiling daily towards achieving his goal of a prosperous future for them all. He begged patience from Angie for a while longer, but she stubbornly carried on with her independent venture at a time when the family struggled.

Around the period that Angie and William were experiencing difficulties, a 17-year-old lad by the name of Theophilus Albert Marryshow left his carpentry apprenticeship to work as a newspaper delivery boy for the anti-colonial newspaper, the *Grenada People*. The paper was owned and edited by William Donovan. Young Marryshow could not have envisaged that he had taken the first step that was destined to lead to a prominent and renowned political career. The year was 1904.

On a hot sunny afternoon in 1905, Angie noticed that two-year-old Iris was not his usual boisterous self as he sat quietly sucking on his thumb. She knew instinctively that all was not well with her toddler son and his hot but damp forehead indicated fever. Angie brewed a cup of the specific herbal tea known for being effective in treating fevers and spooned it to her son, before putting him down for a nap. A short while later, Angie checked on Iris and discovered that he was not breathing. She screamed out for help, but it was already too late. Everyone in the community was shocked and saddened to hear that the endearing little man had been so suddenly taken. William in particular was devastated and wept uncontrollably. Angie was numb with grief.

William and Angie remained inconsolable and for some time following Iris's burial, struggled to cope with daily routines. But support and assistance had been reliably forthcoming from sympathetic relatives and friends.

As twins, Clarice and Iris were uniquely bonded and enjoyed playing together. William explained to his little daughter that Iris had gone to be with the Angels, but Clarice remained traumatised by the absence of her brother, and for a considerable period would run around the house and yard in search of her twin, while tearfully calling his name.

UPWARD AND ONWARD

In spite of the grief of losing a beloved son, William maintained focus on his project and eventually arrived at the point where sufficient progress had been made for kick-starting his new business enterprise. William kissed his family goodbye and headed off on a journey across the sea with his cargo of cola-nuts, cocoa and spices such as cinnamon, cloves, mace, ginger and turmeric. Aware of the significance of her husband's first business trip abroad, Angie prayed that his dealings would be successful.

William was pleasantly surprised by the initial positive response his products received from retailers in Trinidad, Barbados and Guyana, who were not hesitant in their purchases. In particular, the cola-nuts were snapped up by representatives of the Coca Cola factory in Trinidad and orders for regular supplies of the product were placed.

Angie was delighted to hear of William's initial business successes. It seemed that at long last things were beginning to take a turn for the better and hopefully in an upward and onward direction. Angie gave thanks to the Almighty.

William's academic background, business experience and competence in book-keeping ensured that the business was being operated smoothly and efficiently. He was the only supplier of cola-nuts in Grenada during a period when the product was in high demand. William also supplied cocoa, nutmeg and various other spices on a regular basis to his foreign customers. He returned to Grenada with a variety of commodities purchased from abroad and sold them to large retail concerns in towns across the island.

William's export and import undertakings successfully filled a gap in the market. He became a well-known and highly respected businessman, not only in Grenada but also neighbouring islands.

William: Successful businessman.

There was a general boom in the island's economy during the first two decades of the 20th century and many small businesses were being established. Angie's half-sister, Da Dab, commonly known as Mrs Jeremiah following her marriage, became the first person in St David's to set up a stall selling refreshments at the Church gate. The aroma of freshly fried fish cakes, breadfruit and bakes would waft through the Church, triggering the rumbling of stomachs, and mouth-watering thoughts of the longed-for scrumptious snacks would obstruct attention to the Sermon. At the eagerly awaited end of the service, members of the congregation jostled each other as they stampeded out of the Church and hurried to be first in line to make their purchase. Mrs Jeremiah's innovative and most welcome enterprise was later developed and expanded into several profitable retail outlets within the parish.

THE EARLY YEARS

The early 1900s had been an era of national pride and patriotism. The nationalistic mood was being spearheaded by the *Grenada People*, which for many years advocated the rights of the people. It had only been three years since Theophilus Albert Marryshow was taken on as a newspaper delivery boy by the Editor, William Donovan, but his exceptional abilities had been recognised, and by the year 1907, the ambitious young Marryshow was already an up-coming Political Writer on the journal.

It was within this heightened spirit of flag-waving that the court case brought against Bob Benjamin in 1907 was closely followed. Mr Benjamin, a black civil servant from the village of Gouyave in the parish of St John, was known nationally for his stance against the Colonial Treasurer, The Honourable Norman Lockhart. Outraged that his office had been demeaned after Lockhart had spoken to him in a disrespectful and derogatory manner, Benjamin responded angrily and impulsively. He pulled out the pistol that had been attached to his belt and shot Lockhart in the hip.

Benjamin was arrested and remanded into custody prior to being taken to the Court House in St George's, where he was charged with grievous assault. He remained in custody until the Proceedings commenced and was pronounced guilty at the end of the trial. Benjamin was sentenced by the Judge to 12 years of imprisonment. The people were furious. They considered the sentence unjustly severe and protested by organising island-wide demonstrations, and petitions signed by thousands were submitted to the judiciary. The vociferousness of the campaign brought about an Appeal Hearing, at the end of which a reduced sentence was granted.

Motor cars arrived for the first time on the island in 1907. It was a momentous day for those in the community who experienced their first sighting of an automobile. Alarmed by unfamiliar sounds, many people hurried onto the road to investigate its source. They were confronted by a large object shuttling along noisily on wheels with thick grey/black smoke bellowing from its rear. The driver was in uniform and two well-dressed white ladies in hats and gloves were seated behind him. Astonishment and horror were closely followed by pandemonium as individuals who witnessed the phenomenon scattered in different directions and dived for cover. Some jumped into the nearest river. Others took refuge within thick bushes or ran panic-stricken into their houses. Riders who came onto the scene were thrown off startled horses as the animals bolted in fright. It had indeed been an amazing spectacle and a sensational topic of conversation and embellished recounting for a considerable period thereafter.

Nothing surpassed what many in the community considered the highlight of 1907. Communities throughout the island buzzed when it was announced that the first ever organised cricket match at Queens Park, St George's, would be held on Whit Monday. Cricket was the most popular sport of the period and the majority looked forward to the event with anticipation and excitement.

William, a long-time cricket enthusiast, set off on horseback at daybreak on the morning of the match with a bag containing food and drink strapped to his horse. There were other riders similarly equipped, but the majority of people from communities across the island undertook the journey to the stadium in St George's on foot. Everyone was intent on arriving early enough to secure a good seat or standing spot that would guarantee a clear view of the match.

The first professionally organised cricket match held at Queens Park was filled with gaiety, wild cheering, beating of drums and eating and drinking. The teams were loudly and enthusiastically supported by the crowd. Every run made or wicket taken was met with thunderous applause and celebratory jigging. At the end of the sporting day, spectators were in joyous mood and danced all the way home in rhythm to calypsos and beating drums. It was, for them, an unforgettable interlude in time.

William's business continued to flourish and by the year 1910, he was the owner of two estates on which his large crop for export purposes was produced by hired workers. William had taken advantage of a law enacted in 1901 enabling the Government to acquire and pay a just price for abandoned estates. These estates were then sold on to those who were able to purchase in cash or subdivided into plots and sold in easy instalments.

Many people in the community were perplexed and suspicious by the sudden and unexpected upturn in the family circumstances. They were not aware that William had been working long and hard to realise his business vision. Nor did they understand the reasons for his frequent trips abroad. Various rumours and speculation into how William's money was acquired were circulated. Most believed was the rumour that he had found a large treasure chest overflowing with money whilst on a visit to a foreign land.

William was passionately interested in the political affairs of the island and very much supported the struggle for self-determination. When a seat became vacant on the District Council, he seized the opportunity for gaining a footing on the political ladder. He applied for nomination but failed to secure the required number of votes when nominees were elected. William's adopted community remained patriotically territorial and were resistant to being represented by a 'foreigner'.

Meanwhile, the ambitious and talented Theophilus Albert Marrryshow had worked his way up to the position of Political Article Writer and Sub-Editor on the *Grenada People*. He was heavily influenced by the newspaper's owner and Editor, William Donovan, who had been campaigning for the removal of Crown Colony since 1883. The association would prove inspirational to Marryshow's future personal endeavours for Caribbean Self-Government and Federation.

Marryshow progressed to being a Writer on the *Chronicle and Gazette*, one of the oldest newspapers in the Caribbean. He co-founded *The West Indian* with his compatriot C. F. P. Renwick in 1915 and his controversial political views were regularly echoed in the newspaper's editorials. A pamphlet entitled 'Cycles of Civilisation', by T. A. Marryshow, published in the year 1917, was applauded not only in Grenada but throughout the Caribbean. It had been written in response to South Africa's President Smuts's derogatory assertions regarding African peoples and civilisations. T. A. Marryshow's future political initiatives would be significantly impactful on the nation's struggle for self-determination and government.

A BRAND NEW HOME

Angie and William were expecting their eighth baby when tragic news of the sinking of the *Titanic* broke on 5th April 1912. The liner, which had set sail from Southampton, England, on 10th April 1912, was the most modern ship of the period and deemed unsinkable. The couple's second daughter Rosie was born in June of that year. Angie was just 28 years of age, but, following the arrival of Ivan, Clarice, Iris and John, had given birth in quick succession to Lloyd, O'Hanley, Mathias and David in 1906, 1907, 1909 and 1910 respectively.

The family home had been extended to accommodate the steadily increasing number of siblings. But in keeping with their significantly improved economic circumstances, William decided in 1913 to commission the building of a home that would suitably reflect their up and coming affluent lifestyle.

The house was built at the top of a small hill on purchased land in the village of Vincennes. The two-floor building was constructed from timber and concrete. There were four large bedrooms on the upper level. The living area on the ground floor consisted of a spacious dining area, large living room and a good sized study. All rooms contained the finest furniture and a grand piano and gramophone stood proudly among various pieces of mahogany furniture in the living area. The windows were draped with net curtains and lanterns hung from the ceiling of the surrounding veranda. A beautiful flower garden was laid at the entrance to the house. The kitchen, bakery and latrine were within separate purpose-built outdoor units. William's general commodities store was situated at the bottom of the hill and stables were erected on the opposite side of the road. It had been the most impressive-looking complex in the village during the period.

The family were delighted with their newly built home and took up residence in July 1913. Angie, who had been heavily pregnant, gave birth to son Lincoln just one month later, in August. But the joy that was generated within the family by their fresh new start was unexpectedly marred by sad losses. Grandpa Tom, Grandma Millie and Cousin B passed away in quick succession. 1913 was also the year that Angie's biological father, Simon, set off for a short visit to Trinidad, but never returned to the land of his birth.

THE GOLDEN YEARS

The revenue for Grenada between 1911 and 1913 exceeded those of previous years. The wealth came from the export of cocoa, nutmegs, mace and cotton seeds, and businesses flourished throughout the island. It was a period when William's name appeared in the Annals of Grenada as an up and coming proprietor from St David's.

William came home from business trips abroad not only with his imported cargo but also a variety of books for the children and gifts including jewellery for his wife. Angie was undeniably always thrilled with the various pieces she received. Angie would reflect on her childhood and the times she wished for pretty gold bangles like those that were presented to her younger sister Alfreda. It seemed almost like a fairytale to Angie that she now possessed more jewellery than she could have ever imagined.

It had indeed been a prosperous period for the family and they enjoyed a comparatively high standard of living. The Radix's became well known not only within the parish of St David's, but throughout the island. Angie and William were among the top-listed socialites of the day and people from their own community and beyond were regularly entertained in their beautiful home.

The couple employed housekeeping staff and a nanny to help care for the younger children. A live-in seamstress was contracted for three months each year to produce new outfits for the entire family. The garments were stitched on a sewing machine that was operated by a foot pedal.

Angie was the respected mistress of the house. She organised and supervised her staff and ensured that their salaries were reliably paid at the end of each month. But Angie was a single-minded woman with aspirations of her own and felt trapped in the condition of being perpetually pregnant. On discovering being yet again with child, Angie would pronounce in exasperation that she was nothing but a 'baby machine'. It was an age when people in the community had no concept of birth control or that it even existed.

Angie: Spirited, single-minded and philanthropic.

Angie gave birth to four more babies following the arrival of Lincoln. They were Daniel, Alban, Eileen and Thomas. But it was ironically the experience of having to deliver Lincoln and Daniel unassisted that inspired a worthwhile career. Angie discovered that she possessed a skill that could be exploited beneficially and after considerable personal deliberation decided that she would set herself up as a community midwife.

Dee Dee was alarmed on hearing of Angie's intended new venture and expressed concern regarding her daughter's capacity to sustain such an endeavour. William, on the other hand, had every faith in his wife and wished her well. He could not help but admire Angie's confidence and self-belief. It was a time when a professional midwifery service was not in existence and babies were delivered by experienced individuals or older members of the extended family.

Angie thought through and prepared methodically before taking up her self-appointed position. She purchased a large bag and filled it with items including a pair of scissors, an enamel basin, carbolic soap, string, towels and boric powder. Boric powder was in those days added to cool boiled water and used for carrying out enemas.

Angie's midwifery service was passed on by word of mouth and within a relatively short period she was being called upon to deliver babies at various times of the day or night. Angie became increasingly skilful and even devised a method of detecting and turning around babies that lay in breech positions in the womb. Angie's post-natal delivery package was innovative for the time. Her patients were monitored for eight consecutive days after giving birth and those who were lethargic or poorly were treated with Angie's home-made remedies. These may be spoonfuls of a mixture containing cod liver oil, goat's milk and black pepper, chicken soup with garlic or large cups of a brewed herb called 'Rotten Mary'. Angie's intervention ended on the eighth day and after she had provided her patient with a warm bath followed by a full body massage. A fee was not required for the service, but various women showed appreciation by offering Angie a six-pence coin or even a solitary safety pin. All offerings were graciously accepted.

Angie's service was available during an era when breast milk was considered an effective treatment for minor ailments and nursing mothers may even be approached and asked to insert droplets of breast milk directly into the eyes of an individual suspected of having an eye infection.

Despite their relative privileges, the Radix family remained integral members of a 'one big family' community. Everyone looked out for each other and generously offered mutual assistance whenever it was required. When Angie and William's youngest son Thomas was accidentally scalded with boiling water, a neighbour volunteered to nurse him back to health. The kindly woman would lift Thomas onto the sofa, before gently coating the burnt areas of his body with a substance extracted from a particular plant known for its soothing and healing components. The treatment was applied on a daily basis until the child's wounds were properly healed.

Angie was herself a magnanimous woman. She cared about the welfare of others and willingly gave to those who asked to 'borrow' but never 'paid back' a few dollars, cupfuls of sugar, spoonfuls of salt, sticks of matches or even a measure of iodine. The children of a young widow were looked after at the house free of cost. Angie's altruism enabled the young mother to support her family by going out to work. When a friend contracted tuberculosis, Angie took in her daughter and paid to have the woman's clothing and bedding laundered each week. Angie often offered advice to battered wives, and homeless unmarried mothers-to-be were temporarily accommodated at the house. Needless to say, the Radix household was at various times very full and lively.

William, who as a child had been the recipient of private tuition and was at one time a teacher, resolved to pass on to the children his interest in books and love of reading. Education was a priority and William desired the best educational and career opportunities for his offspring. He ensured that the new house contained a study and its shelves were stacked with novels, encyclopaedias, manuals and journals. It had been a quiet place for reading, writing or school work and would prove advantageous to future educational and career aspirations.

Children of the age continued to attend the school house in St David's proper that was once visited by Angie's grandmother, Hope. But teaching methods had since progressed. A wider curriculum had been put into place and there was a significant increase in the number of children being educated on a daily basis.

SIGNIFICANT EVENTS, 1914-1918

When the First World War broke in the year 1914, a large number of young men considered volunteering their services to England, which at that time was called 'the Mother Country'. The feasibility of William making a viable contribution towards the war effort was discussed and dismissed. William and Angie decided that, at 38 years of age, William would be too old. Furthermore, the couple were at that point parents to seven young children and family commitments had to take precedence. But Joseph Wiltshire Fletcher, an assistant teacher at the school the children attended, was among 150 men who left Grenada in 1915. The men joined the British West Indian Regiment en route to fight alongside the Allies against Germany.

In the year 1916, roads from St George's to Sauteurs via St David's and Grenville were covered in tarmac. By the following year there were approximately 150 vehicles on the new tarmac roads. William, a conservative man, was wary of the new motor invention. He decided to leave the cars to the younger generation and continued to travel around the island on horseback.

In the year 1917, William and Angie's seven-year-old son, David, passed away after a brief illness. It was not unusual in those days for children to pick up deadly viruses, but there were no antibiotic drugs or vaccines to treat or prevent highly infectious diseases. David had been a beautiful, intelligent and charismatic child and was sadly missed by the family and all who knew him.

Angie and William's second surviving son, John, won a scholarship to attend Mount St Benedict's College on the island of Trinidad in 1918. A Scholarship Ordinance had been passed in 1916 and John, aged just 13, was at the time the youngest person in Grenada to have won a scholarship to enter into higher education. The family were elated and proud.

But John, a bright boy who always showed more interest in books than play, received encouragement and assistance from William during many weeks of studying prior to sitting his examinations. He also benefited from the reading material that had been put into place by his father.

Soon, preparations were underway for John's departure. Angie, whose sons were always well groomed and smartly outfitted, was determined that John would be one of the best dressed boys at the college. And sure enough, John left Grenada en route to Trinidad dressed in his first pair of perfectly creased khaki long pants, crisply starched and ironed white short-sleeved shirt and white boots and socks. He carried a 'grip' packed with newly made items of clothing.

William accompanied his son on the boat journey to Trinidad. Angie stood on the pier and tearfully waved her boy goodbye. She watched with heavy heart as the vessel sailed out of view. Although immensely proud of John's academic achievement, Angie was nonetheless worried and questioned whether he should be living away from home at the tender age of 13. She prayed that God would watch over her son and keep him safe.

Angie was distracted when a female bystander, who witnessed her distress, asked if John was her husband. Angie was dumbfounded, but responded with loud laughter. She was at the time 34 years of age with ten surviving children. It was praise indeed that she appeared young enough to be mistaken for being the wife of her 13-year-old son. Her spirits were immediately lifted.

After ensuring that John was settled at the boarding college, William returned home with an idea. He suggested to Angie that Clarice, a bright and intelligent 15-year-old, should also have the opportunity of a higher education. Angie was in full agreement and a fee-paying place at a reputable college on the island of Trinidad was some time later secured for their daughter. It was arranged that Clarice would board at the home of Angie's cousin, Mrs Feffin Chang, during term time. Feffin was the daughter of Dee Dee's youngest sister May, who had been taken to Trinidad as a baby by their mother Hope in 1875.

Clarice set off for Trinidad accompanied by her mother. She carried a neatly packed suitcase filled with an array of embroidered underwear, night gowns and beautifully made dresses; and, in particular, a brand new sailor suit which was 'reigning', an expression commonly used for defining the most fashionable 'must have' for trendy young girls of the day.

On arrival at Feffin's modest house, Angie's heart sank. She was disappointed to find that her cousin's living conditions fell far below those of the family in Grenada. But during her short stay on the island Angie visited her grandmother Hope and Auntie May, who at the time of the visit was living with and caring for her then elderly mother. Despite her frailty, Hope had retained her faculties and engaged enthusiastically in chatter about the folk back home. She expressed happiness that both Dee Dee and Angie had married well, but commented that men in her day were 'no good'. There was also plenty of humour and eating and drinking. The coming together of the different branches of the family had been a gratifying and enjoyable experience for everyone.

Both Angie and Clarice were most impressed by the beautiful outfits and glittering jewellery worn by their Trinidadian relatives. But Angie decided against placing her precious daughter in an environment that she was not totally satisfied with and returned home with her girl in tow. Clarice sorely regretted not being on the island long enough to have had the opportunity to wear and show off her treasured tailor suit and was, as a consequence, not a happy bunny.

Soldiers who left Grenada in 1915 to join The West Indian Regiment en route to fight with the British against the Germans were not triumphant on their return home after the war ended in 1918. They reported that their Regiment had been segregated, banned from the front line and that individuals had been referred to as 'boy'. The West Indian regiment received lower wages and were allocated menial tasks, such as digging trenches, cleaning latrines and washing linen. The men's account of their war experiences was featured in the nation's newspapers and the people were shocked and outraged that their brave soldiers had been treated with such contempt by those for whom they were willing to risk their lives.

After the end of the war, the doors of the United States of America were opened to anyone from the Caribbean who wished to emigrate. It was the beginning of emigration to the United States by large numbers of Grenadians in search of new opportunities in a modern and prosperous world.

William thought long and hard about moving the family to America, but Angie held fast against it. She had no desire to leave her network of family and close friends for the unknown. William had been a respectful husband who endeavoured to maintain a partnership relationship with his wife. He rarely made a decision without first discussing it with Angie, who, on this issue, was allowed final sway.

THE MARITAL RELATIONSHIP

Although William was overall a reasonable husband, he nonetheless exercised control when it came to the people with whom Angie formed friendships. He monitored her friends and she was not permitted to associate with women he considered 'good-time girls' and, in his view, may lead her astray. William even demanded that Angie got rid of her best friend after deciding that the woman was 'too bright' and therefore likely to impose negative influences onto his wife.

Angie, on the other hand, had her own suspicions regarding William's alleged conduct. Rumours persisted that he was being flirtatious with young girls in the locality; and in particular the very ones he labelled undesirable 'good-timers'. When interrogated by Angie, William always pleaded innocent. He was in truth a normal red-blooded man with

Extraordinary couple: Angie and William Radix.

an eye for a pretty young girl. This was borne out when suddenly one day William announced his intention to marry Mrs Guillame, a well-known attractive young widow in the vicinity, following Angie's demise. He could not have foreseen that Angie was destined to outlive them both by twenty years and more.

Angie and William were essentially a well-connected couple who shared a close and loving relationship. Their nights were filled with passionate embraces and every morning William would take a freshly made cup of coffee to his contented wife before leaving for work. Only the best was good enough for William's true love. She was lavished with expensive gifts and others were employed to do her bidding.

At least one explosive episode may occur during the course of any happy marriage and with William and Angie it started with a minor disagreement that escalated into a heated argument. During their altercation, William called his wife 'a damn fool'. "You mean you left your home in Bocca and came all the way to St David's to marry a fool?" Angie retaliated. That was too much for William and he slapped her hard across the face. Physically stung and emotionally bruised, Angie planned her revenge. A few days later, while William was using both hands to shift a heavy object, Angie pelted him with a sharp stone which struck his forehead and drew blood. Horrified by the reality of her action, Angie panicked, dashed through the front door and ran all the way to her mother's house in Dudmar.

Dee Dee was pleased to see her daughter, but questioned her breathless and unexpected presence. There was no reason for Dee Dee to doubt Angie's plausible explanation that she had been feeling exhausted and needed a break. Mother and daughter chatted and ate lunch together. At approximately 4pm, Dee Dee suggested to Angie that it was time for her to be heading home, but Angie announced to her surprised mother that she would be staying overnight. Dee Dee would hear none of it. She insisted that Angie returned to her family and marched her back home.

On arrival, Angie entered the house hesitantly and was apprehensive about the reception she would receive. It was, as anticipated, a silent and frosty welcome. Everyone kept quiet and her presence was not acknowledged. That night, William avoided the marital bed and chose to sleep on the sofa downstairs. The atmosphere remained frosty until the following Sunday morning, after the children had left for Church. Angie was in the kitchen frying fishcakes in preparation for breakfast when William crept up behind her. He slipped an arm around her waist and asked humbly, "Can I sample one of your fishcakes?" "Of course!" Angie replied light-heartedly, concealing feelings of relief that the ice had finally been broken. She knew that bursting open her husband's forehead with a stone had been a step too far, but somehow felt unable to apologise for her action.

William ate a fishcake or two, kissed Angie on the cheek and praised her cooking. But, in a calm fashion, he went on to reprimand his wife for causing the injury which drew blood. William admitted being too embarrassed to reveal the truth to anyone who enquired into his wounded and swollen forehead. A man being struck by his wife was unheard of in those days and William feared being the butt of ridicule or the subject of embellished and humorous gossip. His offer of an olive branch in return for peace and harmony within the marriage was testament to the deep love and respect he held for his wife.

PARENTING STYLES

William and Angie's parenting of their offspring was modelled on methods passed down the generations. Angie maintained responsibility for the day-to-day running of home and family. William worked to provide financial support.

Angie managed the children with military precision that was not dissimilar to a Sergeant-Major in the Army, and the rod certainly did the talking. Daily routines were structured and gauged by a large chiming clock that hung on the wall in the dining room. Meals were always strictly on time. The siblings had to be in bed by 7.00pm and up for morning prayers at 5.00am. Everyone was expected to be washed, dressed and ready for breakfast by 7.30am before leaving for school at 8 o'clock sharp. They were not permitted to loiter on the road or around shops and whistling and the singing of calypsos were strictly forbidden.

Lincoln may have temporarily forgotten the rule as he unwittingly sang the latest calypso of the day and moved his hips in time to the rhythm while roasting corn on an open fire. He was suddenly and unexpectedly stung by a sharp clip around the ear which almost knocked him off his feet. Lincoln turned around, to be confronted by his angry mother. "Where yuh pick it up?" she demanded harshly. Taken by surprise, Lincoln became flustered and was not immediately aware that he had broken one of the rules by singing a calypso. He assumed that Angie was referring to the corn and replied: "There", nervously pointing to the basket on the ground beside him. Everyone present immediately broke into hysterical laughter. The incident remained a standing joke within the family for quite some time afterwards.

Apart from Sunday, occasions on which the children received special treats were rigidly scheduled with specific menus and occurred at Christmas, Easter and harvest time.

The children always looked forward to Christmas, which seemed to take forever to arrive as the months dragged on. The family was presented with a leg of cured ham and a bottle of wine from W. E. Julien each year during the Christmas season. Mr Julien was the proprietor of a large firm in St George's with which William procured business deals.

Angie ensured that the gifted ham was stored safely in an alcove near the ceiling that could not be easily reached. But the older boys would climb to wherever the ham was placed and help themselves to large bites of the delicious salted meat. When it was eventually brought down in preparation for Christmas, Angie was always horrified to find it ravished. She would shake her head in frustrated disbelief and declare that, regardless of how safely the ham was secured, mice always succeeded in sniffing it out! But after prolonged and thorough cooking, a portion would be cut into slices and distributed among the neighbours.

Many years passed before 'the penny dropped'. Angie realised that the despised mice were actually her very own mischievous sons when the Christmas ham remained untouched year on year after they had all left home!

Before retiring to bed on Christmas Eve, Angie handed each child a stocking for hanging. The siblings woke at 5.00am on Christmas morning and would be filled with excited expectations about the day ahead. But, like every other day, Christmas was also strictly scheduled. It started with prayers, followed by everyone joining in the singing of at least two Christmas carols. They would afterwards get washed and dressed and be seated on the two long benches that faced the wooden table in the dining room in readiness for breakfast at 7.30am. Christmas breakfast usually consisted of fried ham, black pudding, eggs and freshly made bread, washed down with 'cocoa tea'. After breakfast had been eaten, the siblings were allowed to take down their stockings and play with the various toys and trinkets within. These may include balloons, spinning tops, marbles, rubber balls, pencils or even a few coins. But, like many children of the day, the boys in particular made their own play instruments from natural resources. These may include catapults from sticks cut from branches; flutes or recorders from bamboo; or wheels extracted from broken bicycles being converted into a hand-propelled vehicle called the 'roller'. It was not uncommon to see an excited youngster, baton in hand, furiously but strategically steering his roller along winding pathways while speeding alongside.

A lavish spread was laid out at lunch on Christmas Day and included pork, chicken, stewed peas and various provisions, followed by sweet potato pudding. Red wine and jugs filled with home-made beverages such as ginger beer and sorrel were also on the table. Coconut buns and crackers with cheese were readily available throughout the day. But ice cream was the favourite treat of the day and enjoyed by all. There was never a shortage of volunteers happy to turn the handle of the tub in which it was made.

Christmas in the Radix household and in many other homes throughout the island was always a time of merriment and indulgence.

The family also celebrated Easter. They all attended Church on Easter Sunday and mutton would be served at lunch. But the siblings particularly looked forward to their 'cook up' on La Sagesse beach on Easter Monday. The day would be spent frolicking on the beach, swimming or engaging in the flying of home-made kites. Kite flying was a seasonal cultural activity enjoyed by youngsters all over the island.

Harvest was an annual social event in the community. It was a popular outdoor function attended by young and old. There were various stalls on which may be sold snacks such as coconut buns or tarts, bread rolls, fishcakes, coconut and guava candy and freshly made ice cream. People were also able to participate in lucky dips and raffles. Angie and William's children were always permitted to take part in harvest and each child received six pence to spend at will. The siblings would set off in happy mood with plenty of humorous banter and playful pushing and jostling on the way. Harvest provided the opportunity to socialise freely with friends and generally have a good time.

The offspring of Angie and William dearly loved their mother and made every effort to please her. But the siblings were rarely kissed or cuddled by their mother and they were afraid of her draconian manner.

William, on the other hand, was a warm-hearted and compassionate father. He disliked the use of corporal punishment and was the parent who comforted the crying babies at night. The children were always happy and relaxed when their father was at home. He would give them his full attention, enquire about their school day, read to them or test their separate abilities in spelling, grammar and maths.

The siblings did not at all times understand their father's grammatically correct diction. Little Rosie particularly looked forward to William coming home at the end of the working day. He often lifted his young daughter onto his lap while coaxing her into telling him all about her day. One evening, Rosie proudly showed off to her father the first yam she produced without assistance from the garden. William was duly impressed and asked jokingly, "Rosie, who dug this nice little yam for you?" "Beg u pardon, Pa?" Rosie replied. "Who dug this nice little yam for you?" he repeated. Rosie was baffled by the word 'dug'. The only 'dug' she could think of was Mrs Doug, who lived across the road. And she emphatically denied receiving any help whatsoever from Mrs Doug. William was amused, but knew that his young daughter, like many others, spoke in present tense but prefixed 'de dig' to indicate past. At that stage, Rosie had no concept of the meaning of 'dug'.

SYNOPSES

As the years went by and the children grew older, their separate characteristic features and behaviours emerged.

Ivan was a pleasant, easy going and intelligent boy who loved sport and was particularly good at cricket. His younger siblings respected and looked up to him because of his 'oldest brother' status. Ivan was the privileged favourite son who took on a meek and helpless persona in the presence of his doting mother. He could do no wrong in her eyes and was showered with love and attention and praised for the smallest achievement. Angie even refused to let her precious boy out of the house during hot periods of the day for fear that his pale and sensitive skin would be damaged by the glare of the sun.

Clarice was a bright, bubbly and intelligent girl who for many years revelled in being the only daughter among six sons. She was the pride and joy of both parents. The brothers loved her and she was kind and caring towards them. Clarice was indeed a friendly and popular girl who was allowed to entertain her numerous friends at the house. She was very much the little princess who wore pretty dresses and embroidered underwear. William purchased a piano on which Clarice received music lessons. She was given the freedom to pursue hobbies such as making cakes and concocting different varieties of fruit jam or 'jelly', as it was known in those days.

John was a conscientious, intelligent and studious boy whose strong and steadfast character lay hidden beneath a humble, unassuming and soft-spoken demeanour. John was the loner among the family. He was an avid reader who spent considerable periods of time in the study, peering over various books, encyclopaedias, papers and journals. William would return from business trips abroad with the new publications of the day and John was usually the first among the siblings to review them. William was proud of his son's love of reading and boasted that the boy had taken after him. John was very rarely chastised by his mother because he said very little and kept out of her way by forever burying his head in a book which seemed to be his only companion. Like William, Angie was supportive of John's love of literature. John frequently told his mother that he would buy her beautiful things when he grew to be a man and provide her with everything she ever wanted.

Lloyd was intelligent and caring, with a strong sense of family. He was resolute in developing a close relationship with both parents and strived for their approval. Unlike the other children, who shied away or distanced themselves from their mother's wrath, Lloyd pushed the boundaries with demonstrative affection and displays of precocious paternalistic concern. He would put an arm around Angie's shoulder while offering help in any way possible or be the first to volunteer whenever assistance was required. Lloyd assumed responsibility for the family whenever William was away from home and insisted on sharing his mother's bed, because he felt that it was his duty to protect her. Angie could not help being won over by her son's well-meaning intentions and allowed him to be the loving and dutiful son he endeavoured to be.

Lloyd stayed close to William when he was at home and put every effort into building strong and meaningful ties with him. He loved nothing more than to work alongside his father whenever the opportunity arose. A close bond developed between them and Lloyd became his father's favourite son and best friend.

O'Hanley, who arrived in 1907, was intelligent, single minded and confrontational. He was sturdily built, physically strong and capable of carrying out any task required of him.

O'Hanley related well with his father, but felt unloved by his mother, who frequently disciplined him with harsh words or whippings. O'Hanley's anger was mostly acted out at school. He was a rebellious and defiant pupil who lashed out at teachers. O'Hanley's unruly behaviour often resulted in his expulsion from the school house, but he would retaliate by bombarding the building with a torrent of large stones, smashing windows in the process.

Angie worried about her 'troublesome' son and attempted to curb his difficult behaviours by punishing him severely with the whip. But the beatings O'Hanley received exacerbated his anger and perpetuated the circle of punishment at home, followed by challenges in the school house.

William did not approve of Angie's stern methods. In his opinion, 'beating the boy' was not the answer. William made a point of praising O'Hanley for everything he did well, such as reading or correctly undertaking any set written work. O'Hanley presented no challenges to his father and sought, at all times, to please him.

In quiet moments, Angie wondered whether O'Hanley's behaviour was caused by the coconut which fell from the tree and landed heavily on his head when he was a small boy. She recalled that he had been 'a good child' before the accident and regularly prayed for a resolution to the problem.

Matthias, commonly known as Tox, was born in 1909. He was a bright child who progressed satisfactorily at school and, unlike his older brother, presented no challenges. Tox was quiet and kept himself to himself, but hc was at the same time deep thinking, calculating and shrewdly observant of the world around him.

Tox craved the nurture that had not been forthcoming from his mother and for a period rebelled by seeking out and stealing money that had been put aside for particular purposes. It may have been a ploy for gaining attention, but none of the children were suspected of being responsible for the theft. Angie could not, with any certainty, lay blame on a particular employee or visitor to the house and was convinced that undertaking an enquiry would be futile. She decided to endeavour to outwit the perpetrator and was successful in safeguarding funds in a place that was never discovered.

After nine long years of producing only sons, William and Angie were blessed with a second daughter. The infant was born on 13th June 1912 and was named Rosie.

Rosie was a sickly baby and the family feared for her survival. For the first two years of her life, Rosie was bed-bound and fed a nutritious milk-based formula. Rosie was just over two years old when, suddenly and unexpectedly, she spoke her first words to the nanny charged with looking after her. "Aggie," she said, "pick me up." The nanny screamed in surprise and sheer delight. Everyone came running to see what had happened and were amazed to hear that little Rosie had spoken for the very first time. Angie and William were overcome with joy and relief and thanked the Good Lord for sparing their child.

From that moment on, Rosie's health steadily improved and she blossomed into a plump, happy and robustly built little 'tomboy'. She possessed a quick wit and was the primary 'joker' among the siblings. As she grew older, Rosie would climb trees, steal mangoes from other people's trees and deliberately pick fights with her contemporaries. Despite being boisterous and mischievous in the company of her peers, Rosie never failed to assume a subdued and compliant persona in her mother's presence. But, like her brothers and sisters, Rosie was less inhibited when William was at home and was favoured and spoilt by him.

Lincoln appeared in 1913. He was the first of five siblings to be born in the family's new home in the village of Vincennes. Lincoln was an inquisitive child with a twinkle in his eyes and a fixed, amused and roguish expression. Lincoln was helpful, always eager to please and would attempt to be in his mother's good books by being one of the first to offer assistance when she asked for it.

Angie and William despaired that Lincoln showed little interest in books or school work. He was frequently caned by the Headmaster for not concentrating on his work and being distracted by the pretty young female teachers. Both parents expressed disapproval when Lincoln's extraordinary behavioural pattern was reported to them, but William was also secretly amused that his son had been so blatantly mesmerised by the opposite sex at such a young age. Angie, on the other hand, was not amused and vowed to 'knock' her son's obsession with girls 'out of him'; but the appliance of corporal punishment failed to bring about the required change.

Angie would have 'hit the roof' if she had known that the smug grin that replaced her son's amused expression was due to the fact that 13-year-old Lincoln had succeeded in enticing an attractive young female teacher into an affair! Such an occurrence was unheard of in an era when teachers were for the most part revered by their students. William would no doubt have been dumbfounded by Lincoln's conquest, but may also have humorously harboured a desire for a few tips from his brazen young son. Angie and William had no idea of their academically unproductive son's true potential. It was yet to be revealed.

Daniel came along in 1915 and was a bright, humorous and active child. He was interested in agriculture and particularly loved planting and reaping potatoes. Daniel was quite unaware of his handsome good looks and was irritated by the attention he received from girls. Daniel preferred hanging with the boys, playing sport, hunting and fishing. He was a high achiever at school and Angie and William were pleased with his progress.

Alban was born in 1917. He was a precocious child who spoke well from an early age. He was inquisitive, constantly asked questions and displayed enthusiasm in getting to know the world around him. Alban developed into a studious boy who was keenly interested in books and reading. He was articulate and showed off his grasp of language by baffling his peers with long words borrowed from the large dictionary slotted alongside other books in the study. Alban's self-imposed air of superiority singled him out to lead every club or organisation in which he was a member. He was head boy at school and also head Scout. Angie and William were proud of Alban. They believed he would join the priesthood after finishing school, because of the dedication displayed in his role as Acolyte at Church.

Eileen was pretty and dainty, with long silky hair. She was born in 1919 and was naughty, demanding and rebelled against having to attend school every day. Eileen loved to wear pretty dresses and have her hair tied with brightly coloured ribbons. She was essentially a little show off who would sing and dance the Charleston at family gatherings. Eileen designed, cut and sewed her first dress at the tender age of seven.

Eileen was eight years old when she was taken by a relative to live in St George's town, but she was not well looked after and very much missed her family and friends in her home village. Eileen was returned home when Angie received word that her youngest daughter was seen in town in a dishevelled state. Eileen was overjoyed to be back in the fold. She became a willing participant at school and achieved well.

Thomas arrived in 1921 and was the last offspring of William and Angie. He was a well behaved and intelligent child who excelled at school. He related well with Eileen and the pair often played together or accompanied each other on fishing trips. Thomas' arrival was not welcomed by his brothers. He was particularly victimised by Alban, who pushed and kicked him for no apparent reason. Despite being bullied or simply ignored by his brothers, Thomas was strong minded and capable of standing his ground. He made sure he received his rightful share of food, which was most important as far as Thomas was concerned, and was not afraid to help himself.

Thomas was just five years old when, on a Saturday morning after Angie had left for town, he began pestering Rosie to cook him not one but two of the eggs that had been put aside for Sunday breakfast. Rosie eventually gave in to her little brother's demands on condition that, if questioned by their mother, he should say that he had not seen anyone help themselves to any of the eggs. Later that day, and as was usually the case, Angie loudly announced her arrival as she entered the gap leading up to the house. Anxious to do right by Rosie and fuelled by a satisfied stomach, Thomas was in high spirits as he sprinted down the hill to greet his mother and bellowed: Nen! Nen! I didn't see anybody take eggs! Didn't see nobody take no eggs!" He had unwittingly given the game away and Rosie cringed with fear as she anticipated their mother's angry response. But Angie could not help being amused by her son's misguided declaration and decided to drop the issue of the missing eggs. Needless to say, Rosie heaved a huge sigh of relief.

A FAMILY COMPLETE

Angie was the happiest of women after the birth of her last child, Thomas. She was hugely relieved that, at 37, her child-bearing years were finally over and declared that there was always an end, even to the longest road. She now looked forward to a happy and contented future, with plenty of time to pursue her personal interests. But fate would deal an unexpected card.

During the period that John was being educated at St Benedict's, holidays were spent with the family. When he was at home, John regularly isolated himself in the Study while concentrating on his assignments. His diligence would be highly rewarded. John returned to Grenada in the year 1922, after successfully completing four years of college education. He was just 17 years old and the family were delighted that their beloved son and brother had passed his final examinations with distinction. William was overcome with pride, while Angie dropped to her knees in thanksgiving. John's achievement was celebrated at the house with family and friends and he was congratulated for his remarkable accomplishment.

Under the conditions of the scholarship, John was required to teach at an appointed school for two years. He was offered a position at a school in the village of Beaulieu. John's achievements thus far had been stepping stones on the road towards fulfilling his ultimate ambition to become a doctor. And it was not too long before he had embarked on a course of study for the examination necessary for gaining entrance into Howard Medical School. Howard was an African-American University in Washington DC.

The year 1922 was not without sadness for the family. Grandma Hope and Tant Cecae both passed away. Dee Dee was particularly sorrowful by the loss of her mother. Hope had been the subject of widespread sensational gossip and speculation when she abandoned her husband and family for an independent life in a foreign land back in 1875. The amazing strength of character and courage she displayed at an age when women were conditioned to accept their lot in life, was quite staggering. Hope's daring undertaking was greatly admired by subsequent generations of women who had heard her story. By the time of her death, Hope had already been recognised as a true heroine by many sisters in the community.

Following the passing of Tant Cecae, Angie supported William's desire that his two nieces, Helen and Florence, should join the family fold. The girls, who had previously lived with their now-deceased grandmother, experienced few difficulties adjusting into the care of their aunt and uncle and related well with the cousins.

Meanwhile, John, with encouragement from his parents, was spending every free moment in the Study, working towards fulfilling his career aspiration. John's efforts had not been applied in vain. He passed the required examination with flying colours and won a place at the Medical School of his choosing. The year was 1924. At that point, older sibling Clarice revealed her ambition for a career. Angie and William desired the best opportunities for their offspring, and readily consented to Clarice accompanying her brother to the United States with the aim of realising her aspirations.

The day arrived when Angie and William stood on the harbour and waved goodbye to Clarice and John as their ship set sail en route to the United States. William felt proud and gratified that the educational foundation that had been put in place for his offspring was beginning to produce dividends. Angie wept and quietly offered a prayer for the safety and welfare of her children in a far away country.

THE DIFFICULT YEARS

The boom in the island's economy during the first two decades of the 20th century was followed by a slump in the early 1920s. Unfortunately for the family, the demand for cola-nuts fell dramatically and seriously impacted on William's once-flourishing export and import business. There appeared to be no respite in the decline and, not long after Clarice and John left for the United States, Angie and William decided to close the business and that William would seek employment in Cuba. It was intended to be a temporary measure pending the recovery of the economy. Lloyd and O'Hanley, the strongest and most robust of the siblings, were chosen to accompany and work alongside their father for the purpose of maximising the family income.

Lloyd, always the patient and dutiful son, gave up his teaching position in favour of the overall good of the family. O'Hanley was a willing participant and viewed the experience as an exciting adventure.

In spite of the depressed economic climate, the 1920s had been an eventful decade for the nation. The first aircraft, a United States flying boat, visited the island in 1924. Three years previously, in the year 1921, Theophilus Albert Marryshow embarked on a one-man mission to the British Parliament. The bold action had been taken in relation to Marryshow's personal struggle with the British for West Indian Self-Government and Federation. The valiant undertaking resulted in the establishment of a partially elective body throughout the British colonised Caribbean being formally approved by the British Government in 1925. T. A. Marryshow was subsequently elected to the Legislature to represent the town of St George. Forty-two years had elapsed since William Galway Donovan initiated the nation's campaign for the removal of Crown Colony and ten years after the baton had been passed on to Theophilus Albert Marryshow, who assumed a wider perspective. The one-time newspaper delivery boy had 'reached'. His long struggle had finally reaped benefits. Marryshow became a revered national hero and was renowned throughout the English-speaking Caribbean. He was the first Grenadian Political Leader to receive such an accolade. Marryshow would retain his political leadership position for 33 years.

The early 1920s was a period of adjustment for Angie. Five members of her family were at that time living away from home and working or studying on foreign soil. Although the days seemed to linger during the children's growing up years, in retrospect Angie realised that the passage between childhood and adulthood was brief and mourned the passing of the years. But she looked forward to receiving and replying to letters from abroad and was pleased to learn that William, Lloyd and O'Hanley had been successful in finding employment.

As anticipated, the men's earnings ensured that the family's lifestyle was being maintained. And Angie and William decided that Rosie, who had been progressing well at school, should be given the opportunity of a secondary education at St Joseph's Convent. Rosie was delighted when Angie revealed the good news.

William was delighted when he received the first of the monthly deliveries of his favourite newspaper, *The West Indian*. Copies of the journal were despatched by a wife who was very much aware of her husband's passionate interest in the political affairs of his country. A grateful William spent much of his leisure time leafing through the pages. He was particularly interested to read the article on T. A. Marryshow's momentous political success and was triumphant. William had been an ardent reader of Marryshow's controversial editorials. He supported his campaign and admired his tenacity.

Rosie was filled with the highest of hopes as she anticipated the arrival of 1926. It was the year that Rosie, aged 13, was scheduled to commence attendance at the prestigious St Joseph's Convent at the beginning of the school term. She could hardly wait to be seen by her peers dressed in her brand-new white blouse, navy blue pleated skirt and navy and white striped tie. The uniform had been carefully ironed and draped on a hanger in Angie's wardrobe in readiness for her first day at the Convent.

Unexpectedly, and before the start of the school term, Angie received a letter from William stating that he was heading home with the boys because he was unwell. He went on to explain that one of his toes had become inflamed. It was slow healing and he was feverish and constantly tired. William felt the need to be cared for by his wife during an intended short period of rest and recovery.

Angie was happy to see her husband and sons after two long years and the children were overjoyed that their father and brothers were home again. As usual, William was armed with jewellery for his wife and books for the siblings. His presence was like a breath of fresh air and the home environment rippled with joy. The youngsters gathered around their father and spoke spontaneously of their individual pursuits and accomplishments. William

William: Devoted husband, loving and inspirational father.

gave them his full attention and made sure that each child was made to feel special.

Eileen and Thomas were particularly happy. The youngest siblings very much missed their father's presence and relished his outpourings of kind words and demonstrative affection.

Meanwhile, Angie listened with interest to Lloyd and O'Hanley's account of their experiences in Cuba. Angie marvelled at how O'Hanley conversed with her in a calm and pleasant manner. It seemed that her once-troubled son may have matured into a reasonable young man.

After the euphoria surrounding the homecoming, Angie, concerned by her husband's drawn and tired appearance, insisted he retired to bed, where she served him with a large bowl of nutritious soup. Angie became alarmed that William groaned loudly and deeply as he slept. She applied her best efforts to cure her husband's ills. She dressed his ulcerated and painful toe, administered tried and tested herbal remedies and provided him with a variety of wholesome stews and soups.

After one week and little sign of improvement, the doctor was called. William received a full examination and liquid medication was prescribed, but there appeared to be no improvement in his condition. Instead, his health steadily deteriorated, and when his breathing became laboured, Angie hurriedly called the children to his side. The family were gathered around the bed and Angie held her husband's hand as he took his last breath. William passed away peacefully in May 1926. He was just 49 years of age and had been home for just two weeks. The family were devastated.

William's funeral was attended by relatives and friends from across the island. A Requiem Mass was held at St David's Catholic Church, followed by a procession to the cemetery at Windsor Forest.

Angie grieved and wore black for two years following William's passing. She placed a large bouquet of flowers at his graveside and sat with him for several hours every Sunday afternoon. Angie was often heard crying as she lay in bed at night, bemoaning the loss of her husband. She missed his comfort and companionship and wished they could have grown old together. Hers was a happy marriage, but Angie felt that William had been taken much too soon. She was just 42 years old and did not relish the thought of having to live what could be many more years without the man she loved by her side. Angie was completely bereft and felt that her heart had been ripped apart.

But Angie was warmed and heartened when she recalled the happy times the couple spent together. She would smile as she thought of how fortunate she had been to be married to an intelligent man of stature who was also caring and considerate. William not only gave Angie his heart, but had elevated her into a life of privilege. Angie would recall childhood experiences. She shared a close relationship with her mother, but had been treated with disparity by her step-father. Only the favoured Alfreda received the desired gifts, but Angie suspected that it may have been her destiny to be showered with plenty by an adoring and generous husband. Angie missed out on schooling because she was on most days required to look after her younger siblings. But William was comparatively well educated and had put into place a sound educational foundation for their children.

Despite the experienced ups and downs, Angie considered herself a blessed woman who had lived the good life. She gave thanks to God for sending her a loyal and devoted husband who had been a responsible, loving and inspirational father to their offspring. Angie lived during a period when a woman's luck was gauged simply by the calibre of the man she was able to catch. And Angie had indeed caught a big fish.

The world is continually revolving, which is predictive of change being the only constant in life. Angie now found herself a single and unsupported mother of six young children and two outstanding mortgages. After many years of glory, it had been a tremendous fall from grace. The staunchly religious Angie sought solace in her Faith and prayed daily for the strength, courage and the spiritual guidance needed to get the family through their time of crisis.

Even though the children were unable to grasp fully the magnitude of the reversal in the family fortune, they were deeply saddened by the loss of their father and missed his warm, loving and reassuring presence. Eileen and Thomas were particularly traumatised. They were just beginning to get to know and form a relationship with their wonderful father and suddenly he was gone. The siblings feared that there would now be no respite from the harsh disciplinarian that was their mother.

All too soon the family's entire savings had been exhausted and mortgage arrears were accumulating. Angie's fears were realised when Bailiffs arrived at the door threatening repossession of the house and its contents. Angie pleaded for a little more time and the mortgage collectors were persuaded to suspend repayments for a fixed short period.

In her endeavour to procure money for settling the family's debt, Angie sold their estates, and every other possession of value was put up for auction. On hearing of the family's plight, W. E. Julien, who was a former business associate of William, stepped in with a magnanimous proposal. He offered to purchase the family home and surrounding land and re-sell the entire property to Angie on an affordable monthly repayment plan. It had been an offer that Angie could not refuse and for which she was immensely grateful. Angie considered the proposal 'God-sent'. It ensured stability for the children and she fell to her knees and thanked God for the Good Samaritan who extended a hand of assistance at a pivotal juncture.

Rosie, who had been anxiously looking forward to attending the highly regarded St Joseph's Convent, dressed in her new crisp uniform, was crushingly disappointed when Angie altogether withdrew her from school. Rosie had boasted to her peers of the intended school transfer and they secretly mocked her downfall. They had been fully aware that if anyone dared to openly tease or ridicule Rosie, she would not hesitate in delivering a hefty cuff directly on the mouth of her tormentor. The decision to take Rosie out of school had not been taken lightly, but Angie could no longer afford paid assistance and Rosie was needed at home to help with routine housekeeping tasks. It included being single-handedly responsible for laundering the clothing and bedding of the entire family on a weekly basis. Rosie would carry large bundles to the river and beat or rub them clean on large stones before drying them in the glare of the sun. Particular items of clothing such as shirts were starched prior to being 'pressed' by a heavy manual iron that was regularly reheated on a simmering coal pot. The laundering process was exhaustive and back-breaking, but the young Rosie remained compliant and uncomplaining.

Each family member was expected to make a contribution, as everyone pulled together during their time of hardship. Lloyd, always the dutiful and dependable son, volunteered to take responsibility for repaying W. E. Julien by seeking employment in Columbia. He was joined by O'Hanley and Tox.

The land was worked by Lincoln and Daniel for producing food. Angie purchased large sacks of flour for baking bread and buns that were sold within the locality. Farm animals were slaughtered by Lincoln and Daniel, and meat and also black pudding were always available for purchase within the community on Saturdays.

Angie was a proud and smartly dressed woman with a graceful gait, and, despite financial constraints, remained steadfast in her values. The children were encouraged to read. Daily school attendance was compulsory and complaints of being unwell were not considered a valid excuse for absence. Each child received exercise books, pencils and a copy of the standard of Royal Reader that was appropriate to their school year. The siblings attended Church each Sunday and were sent to Confession and received Holy Communion once a month.

Lincoln, Daniel and Alban continued their membership of the Scouts, but their shirts were no longer cut from the best material and stitched by a skilled seamstress. They were now being cut from sacks that had once contained flour and stitched by their mother. Angie also patched outgrown items of clothing into various outfits for the growing siblings. It had been quite a come-down in the family's circumstance, but Angie soldiered on with fortitude.

News of Clarice's marriage and pregnancy just three months following William's demise was received with shock and disappointment. Clarice had been sent to America two years previously to pursue a career and Angie was disheartened that her daughter had followed a different path. But she could do nothing but accept what was totally out of her control. Angie came to the conclusion that the turn of events was meant to be and that William's passing enabled 'a soul' for their first grandchild. This was a culturally held belief related to the circle of life.

The latter half of the 1920s was a period of significant modernisation on the island. Telephone lines were widely installed in the year 1927. A central water authority was established in 1928 and electric lights were for the first time switched on in the town of St George also that year.

One of the important events that occurred within the family during 1928 was the marriage of Ivan to his childhood sweetheart. But Angie's happiness for the young couple was tinged with feelings of sadness that she may have lost primary status in the affections of her favourite son.

Everyone was overjoyed when much-loved daughter and sister, Clarice, visited the family with her two toddler daughters in December 1928, four years after leaving for the United States. Faced with the reality of the changes in the family's circumstances, Clarice was shocked and upset. The young family arrived during the Christmas period and Clarice's distress was alleviated by the celebrations that were essentially as she remembered them to be. Christmas stockings were hung and filled with various toys and trinkets. The menu included favourite foods such as ham, black pudding and pork. There was an abundance of fresh bread and buns. And ice cream remained the favourite treat. It was just like the old days.

During her stay on the island, Clarice spent quality time with the family, rekindled old friendships and enjoyed relaxing on her favourite stretch of beach in La Sagesse. She realised that, despite economic setbacks, hearts and minds could not be changed; and that fundamental family values, principles and expectations remained un-shifted.

Clarice returned to New York, leaving behind her young daughters in the care of their grandmother.

In 1929 the Stock Market crashed in the United States and the ensuing Depression reverberated across the Caribbean and worsened the already difficult economic climate on the island.

The 1920s had been a decade of heartache, loss and struggle as the family experienced the total collapse of their privileged lifestyle. The difficulties, primarily caused by the down-turn in the island's economy, were compounded by William's untimely passing and also the recession that had taken hold in the United States.

Despite the problems encountered, Angie remained a pillar in the locality and worked diligently for the good of the community. She was head of the Rosary Club and prayer meetings were regularly held at the house. Rosie and Eileen were tasked with looking after the grandchildren whenever Angie was called upon to deliver babies or was busy providing her post-natal package of care. Angie also spent a considerable amount of time raising funds for the construction of a local school. It was at a time when nearly every parent in the community was aware of the value of education and the majority of children attended school. The project had been enthusiastically supported by the community at large and there was a swirl of personal contributions. Various women donated from the proceeds of selling homemade buns, tarts or candy. And many men provided labouring assistance during the building process.

On completion of the project, the community gathered in large numbers to commemorate the opening, in 1930, of the first school for young children in the village of Vincennes. It was a historic occasion and a great sense of pride and accomplishment was shared by all.

The first year of the new decade was indeed eventful for the Parish, as it was also in 1930 that the first bus service between St David's and St George's came into operation. It had been the initiative of Angie's nephew, Elias, eldest son of her half-sister Da Da. Elias inherited his mother's entrepreneur spirit with increased vision and enthusiasm. He became the driving force behind the expansion of the Jeremiah's business empire. But suspicions were rife regarding Elias's continued successes during a period of recession when the majority struggled. It was widely rumoured and believed within the largely suspicious and superstitious community that Elias was 'dealing with the devil' and that he had relinquished his soul to Satan in return for success and prosperity.

It was also in the year 1930 that Angie received a letter from Lloyd informing her of his intention to marry a girl who was expecting his child. Angie was having none of it and in her reply expressed disapproval and demanded Lloyd's immediate return home. Lloyd, who would not even consider disobeying his mother, returned as directed and Angie was happy that her son was back where he belonged. Before too long Lloyd had secured a teaching position, but within only a few months disclosed to Angie his long-held ambition of becoming a dentist. Always the dutiful and responsible son, Lloyd feared letting the family down by even thinking of revealing a personal ambition and was consumed with feelings of guilt.

Angie had been very much aware of the sacrifices that her reliable, hardworking and patient son had made for the family and felt that the time had come for Lloyd to put his personal interests first. He had earned it. Angie did not hesitate in offering full support to Lloyd and suggested that the process of gaining entry into Dental School should commence without delay.

Encouraged by his mother's approval and support, Lloyd went on to successfully sit the required examination under the island's Scholarships Ordinance. He left Grenada during the latter half of 1930 for Howard University in the United States, where he had been accepted for studying Dentistry. Lloyd would embark on a similar regime of work and study as his brother John before him.

SIGNIFICANT EVENTS, 1930-1939

The routines of family life in the Radix household in Vincennes, St David's, continued; but by the mid-1930s Angie was caring for five grandchildren who had all been born in the United States. The children's mother, Clarice, posted large parcels from America filled with a variety of items such as beautiful dresses, shoes and various household commodities. In one such box was a bag containing a large quantity of a never-before-seen grainy white powder. After considerable thought, Angie reasoned that the mystery powder had to be some form of porridge oats and decided to sample it one morning. After boiling milk flavoured with cinnamon sticks in a large saucepan, Angie proceeded to slowly mix-in cupfuls of the white substance, but was alarmed by the large bubbles that rose high above the pot and the soapy aroma. She scooped a spoonful for tasting, but spat it out immediately and called out to Rosie and Eileen. The girls hurried to the kitchen, where their mother was standing, wooden spoon in hand. They were invited to taste and offer a verdict, but they also were horrified and mystified. They had never before tasted anything like it and the women decided unanimously that the soap-flavoured 'porridge' should be discarded. A few days later, a letter arrived from Clarice detailing the contents of the parcel which stated that it included powder detergent for washing clothes. The women were momentarily stunned into silence, before collapsing into hysterical and prolonged laughter. Their introduction to washing detergent was an experience that was never forgotten.

Rosie and Eileen, who regularly assisted with caring for their young nephew and nieces and also with housekeeping chores, very much desired to join the Girl Guides, but were forbidden. Both girls felt that their mother had unfairly refused their request, as the boys had all been permitted to be Scout members. Rosie was particularly aggrieved. She felt that she had drawn the short straw, having also missed out on being a pupil at St Joseph's Convent. But Angie offered a consolation prize which took the form of arranging piano lessons for Rosie and both sisters received professional training in dressmaking and general needlework, including embroidering.

After eight long years of study, including medical internship at a hospital in Washington, DC, John returned to Grenada in 1932 a qualified doctor. The family were elated. It had indeed been an occasion for celebration and a gathering of close relatives and friends was organised at the house. The party began with prayers of thanksgiving for John's success and thoughts were expressed regarding the sad absence of William who would no doubt have been extremely proud of his boy. There was clinking of glasses as everyone cheered and toasted the young physician. It was a time when doctors were generally held in high esteem and to have one within the family was considered a remarkable accomplishment.

It had been a happy and congratulatory occasion, with plenty of food and drink, but John was savouring a surprise. The party was in full swing when John took Angie's hand, led her to the centre of the room and asked for silence. He proceeded to make a short but heartfelt speech thanking Angie for always supporting his desire to study. John expressed regret that his beloved father, who had provided an educational platform, was not around to share in his success. At the end of his little speech, John presented his mother with a beautiful box fixed into place with colourful ribbons tied in a bow. A surprised and delighted Angie clasped both hands to her chest before extending them to accept the gift. Everyone held their breath in anxious anticipation as Angie opened the package and withdrew a pair of gold bracelets and a gold chain, on which hung a pendant of precious stone. The silence was broken with a chorus of loud gasps, followed by simultaneous clapping and cheering. John had kept the promise made to his mother when he was just a small boy.

He said at the time that he would give her beautiful things when he grew to be a man. Angie was overcome with joy and pleasure and embraced her son in appreciation.

On the following Sunday, Angie carried a large bouquet of flowers to William's grave and told him of John's extraordinary achievement. She knew that her husband was the proudest of fathers, wherever he was.

John went on to become a popular and well-respected physician across the island. He was an empathetic and compassionate practitioner and, like many other doctors of the day, did not hesitate to rise from his bed in the middle of the night to attend to emergencies. He was also willing to accept offerings of the choicest fruit or vegetables gathered from the gardens of those unable to afford medical fees. John's manner was calm and reassuring and he became known as 'Dr Dear'. The endearment 'dear' was regularly used when addressing his female patients.

John was a generous son and brother who ensured that the family's circumstances were alleviated by providing them with financial assistance. Angie was rejuvenated by the many gifts she received from John, such as gold rings, fashionable dresses with matching hats, elegant shoes and styled wigs. She enjoyed dressing up and in her words 'cutting a dash'. And there was a noticeable spring in her step.

The family home was usually filled with music from records played on their wind-up gramophone on Sunday afternoons. But after a radio was delivered by John, listening to the transmission of American swing bands and popular jazz songs of the day became a favourite pastime. Radio was introduced on the island in the mid-1930s.

John had been for two years a popular medical physician on the island when he married his 17-year-old sweetheart in 1934. Even so, the welfare of his birth family continued to be a priority.

Lloyd returned a fully qualified dentist in the year 1937. Angie cried with happiness and thanked God for the deserved achievement of her altruistic son, who had worked so arduously for his family. Like his brother John, Lloyd's successful homecoming was joyfully celebrated at the house with family and friends. Angie could hardly wait to visit William's grave and tell him of the accomplishment of his favourite son.

Lloyd too showered gifts on his mother. He carried out her very first dental overhaul and a frontal gap was capped with a gold tooth. Angie's mouth was refreshed. Her personal image was enhanced and she never missed an opportunity to confidently flash her newly acquired golden smile.

Lloyd went on to become a popular dental practitioner in Grenada and also on the island of Trinidad.

Meanwhile, Lincoln, who had been deemed a failure, suddenly began spending considerable periods reading in the Study. Teachers were amazed by Lincoln's increased level of concentration during lessons and the unforeseen remarkable progress he was suddenly making in leaps and bounds. To everyone's surprise, Lincoln went on to achieve a 'first' in the end-of-school examinations. Angie in particular was staggered by her son's unexpected enthusiasm for learning. Because of his historical disinterest in school work and reading, she was unaware that he possessed any underlying academic potential and actually considered him 'dim'. Angie could not help being happy and relieved that she had been proven wrong. Lincoln entered Pharmaceutical College in 1932, when he was just 18 years of age. He sailed through the required stages of the training and passed out as a Pharmacist three years later in 1935. It was once more an occasion for celebration. When Angie visited William's grave and spoke to him of their son's success, she sensed that Lincoln's astonishing academic turn-around had been a most welcome surprise for the beloved departed.

Lincoln had been an admirer and pursuer of young women, but they admired his handsome younger brother Daniel. Daniel showed little interest in girls and thought of them as annoying distractions that were best ignored; until, that is, sexual desires kicked in during adolescence and with it a complete change of heart. Daniel suddenly realised that his peers may not have been joking when they teased him for being a 'pretty boy' and decided to capitalise on his 'God-given' physical attributes. Daniel wasted no time in making up for lost time and transformed himself into a charismatic charmer of young women. He purchased a motorbike and used it to impress and excite the girls as he zoomed through various villages and towns. They would giggle and flirt in his presence and compete with each other for his undivided attention. Needless to say, there was never a shortage of easily acquired girlfriends and Daniel was flattered into thinking himself as somewhat of a Don Juan. Nicknamed 'The Darling Hero', he was also a key member of the local 'in crowd' and his friends were regularly entertained at the family home.

Daniel was academically bright and also a gifted creative writer whose articles and poems had been published in some of the newspapers of the day. But Daniel remained keenly interested in gardening and was employed in the agricultural field after leaving school. Influenced by his brothers' professional achievements, Daniel, at age 29, gained entry to a university in America, where he studied Ophthalmology.

Daniel returned to Grenada after completing his studies and opened an Optical Practice in St George's town, while residing with his wife and family in the village of Corinth, St David's. But agriculture was always in Daniel's blood and he eventually abandoned his flourishing Practise and resumed an agricultural career in his beloved country community.

Alban was intelligent and focused. He was also fussy and fastidious and often complained that his young nieces and nephew being cared for by Angie 'messed up' the house. Alban insisted that his shirts were thoroughly washed, starched and smoothly ironed by Rosie. And if he was not present at meal times, his share of food had to be attractively placed on a dish, fully covered and set aside pending his return.

Alban was articulate and often spoke in pompous tones littered with big words. He was indeed 'full of himself' and showed off, to anyone willing to lend an ear, his knowledge relating to procedures within the House of Lords and House of Parliament in London, England. Alban's teachers were impressed by his intelligence and the commanding presence he carried. They predicted that he would have a bright future.

At age 16 in 1933, Alban was appointed to teach at the Roman Catholic School in St David's proper and at all times presented for work smartly dressed in jacket and tie. He was subsequently successful in obtaining a teaching position at Belmont Roman Catholic School on the island of Trinidad, which he held from 1934 until 1937.

The coronation of George V1 in May 1937 was commemorated with patriotism by the nation. Despite being granted partial self-government, Grenada remained a British colony. It was the basis on which the people believed themselves to be British. The coronation of the new British King was marked with firework displays, dancing in the streets and cook-ups on the beach. The Governor drove around the island and addressed school children gathered at pre-determined points. The youngsters had been given three days' recess from school and were required to march before the Governor and salute the British flag.

Lincoln and Rosie both married in 1938, and Alban departed to the United States to study Law. Of Angie's 12 surviving children, only Eileen and Thomas were at that stage still residing at the family home.

The family was hit by a wave of sadness when, also in 1938, Dee Dee's husband of many years, Pa Way, passed peacefully in his sleep. He had been a responsible and dependable husband and father and was sorely missed by the entire relatives and friends alike.

Meanwhile, Ivan continued being the easy-going and light-hearted son and brother with an ever-ready chuckle. He was a contented soul with no driving ambition or aspiration and was not particularly impressed by his brothers' professional accomplishments. Ivan cruised through life, happy in his occupation as a shopkeeper and his days were largely spent engaging in hilarious banter with passers-by or customers whose purchases were made mainly on a buy now, pay later agreement. But there were no worries. People in those days were generally honest and trustworthy. Ivan never lost the status of being his mother's favourite son. Even though he was a grown man and married too, he continued to play the 'little boy' role in Angie's presence and she seemed unable to overcome her need to spoil and mollycoddle her 'forever baby'. Ivan was also adored and pampered by his wife and loved and respected by his younger siblings. He was well adjusted, at peace with himself and enjoyed the simple life.

The family heard nothing from O'Hanley and Matthias, who had been working in Columbia since 1926. Angie worried constantly about her sons' well-being and prayed each day for their safety and welfare.

After less than a year of marriage, Lincoln became restless and decided that the marital institution was not for him. He felt that he had not yet fulfilled his career potential and consequently had not been fully stretched. In 1939, Lincoln followed in John's footsteps by successfully gaining entry into Howard Medical School in Washington, DC. He too would become a working student.

Shortly after Lincoln left for America and at Clarice's request, Angie uprooted the family and moved to a house in St George's town. The property had been purchased by Clarice after she had successfully obtained places for her daughters at St Joseph's Convent. She was also of the view that the comparative sophistication of life in the island's main town should prove beneficial to the rounded development of the siblings.

Significantly for Grenadians, 1939 was the year that the first passenger bus service linking all towns came into operation. Water pipes were also for the first time plumbed throughout the island.

On 3rd September 1939, the nation was alerted to the outbreak of the Second World War by continuous tolling of Church bells in every parish. A large number of young men joined the Grenada Reserve Force and guarded strategic points in conformity with the defence protocol of the island. Others enlisted in either the British or Canadian armed forces. Angie's youngest son, Thomas, joined the British Merchant Navy.

The beginning of the war came at a time when Angie and the children were adjusting to their new life in the town of St George, but Angie remained a country girl at heart. She maintained her house in Vincennes and regularly spent weekends there. During visits to the country, Angie would tend her garden, visit William's grave and catch up with family and friends. She always returned to town carrying an abundance of produce reaped from her garden, some of which was distributed among the new neighbours.

John: Studious, conscientious and benevolent.

Scout group – St David's, 1933: Alban is seated middle row, second from left.

Lloyd: Intelligent, principled and dependable.

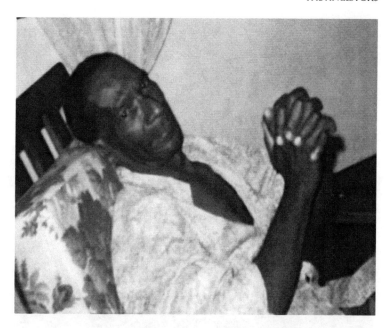

Daniel: Talented, charismatic and self-assured.

Alban: Scholarly, pompous and self-absorbed.

Ivan: Easy-going, contented soul.

Thomas and Lincoln standing at back. Alban and Clarice seated.

Angie surrounded by siblings; from left, Eileen, Thomas and Rosie.

Alban.

Eileen: Dressed in one of her favourite creations.

Rosie: Warm-hearted, quick-witted and uncomplaining.

Lincoln: Vibrant and driven.

Eileen: Aged 17, 1936

THE FINAL YEARS

New Year 1940 was greeted by the nation with some trepidation. It was war-time and the future was uncertain. The year started with sadness for the family. Ivan lost his beloved wife after a long illness. He was devastated, but several months later found comfort in the arms of a long-standing family friend. Less than two years after the sad passing of his first wife, Ivan announced his intention to marry for the second time. Angie was dismayed that Ivan would even consider remarrying so soon after the demise of a very dear daughter-in-law. But, in spite of his mother's expressed reservations, Ivan's mind had been made up and he married his newly found love in 1941.

During the war years the nation experienced shortages in imported products such as petrol, kerosene, matches, flour, salt and butter. It was a period when Grenadians migrated in large numbers to Trinidad, Curacao or Aruba in search of economic opportunities.

Following the bombing of Pearl Harbour by the Japanese in 1942, shipments of nutmegs from the Far East to Europe and North America ceased. Grenada nutmeg was, as a consequence, highly demanded and prices soared. It was a lucrative period not only for established nutmeg dealers but also ordinary folk, whose primary income was dependent on the sale of their nutmeg crop.

There was a national sense of pride that Grenada was at last catching up with the modern word when the island's first airport was opened at Pearls in 1943. The airfield had been the result of a 1942-signed agreement between Britain and the United States to obtain land for airbases on specific Caribbean islands in exchange for destroyers and the construction of airfields.

Meanwhile, Angie continued to manage her home and family with a firm hand and very little compassion. She ensured that the grandchildren were healthy, well cared for and conservatively dressed. They attended school regularly and made excellent progress. But even though they were generally well behaved, the girls would be physically chastised for the smallest actual or unintended misdemeanour. Only the favoured grandson was spared. Angie was nonetheless deeply upset when, in 1944, the older girls left Grenada to join their mother, Clarice, in the United States.

Just weeks following her grand-daughters' departure, Angie was cheered by the return of Alban. He had applied and was successful in being called to the Bar following qualification as a lawyer in the United States. He was at the time 27 years of age. Alban, who had always been keenly interested in British Law and Legal Procedures, had fulfilled his ultimate ambition by passing the British Bar. It was proof to those who dismissed him as being nothing but fanciful and pretentious, that his highbrow assertions had indeed been knowledge-based and credible. Alban's outstanding accomplishment was acknowledged by relatives and friends, who gathered to welcome him home. Very few students whose education had been largely elementary and delivered in one-room school houses in small Caribbean country communities succeeded alongside advantaged British scholars in the United Kingdom. Angie would once more offer a prayer of thanksgiving. She was particularly grateful for her son's safe return and that he had maintained good health.

Alban was for many years a Barrister of high regard in Grenada, before moving his practice to St Vincent in the late 1950s. He married a Vincentian girl and thereafter became established as a well-known and respected lawyer in his adopted country.

The year 1944 would be forever remembered by the nation for the mysterious disappearance of a boat called *The Island Queen. The Island Queen* had set off in August of that year on a pleasure cruise to St Vincent with a cargo of the brightest, most beautiful and privileged young Grenadians of the day, but failed to reach its destination. Subsequent extensive land and sea searches produced no evidence of the vessel's fate. It had been an unbelievably shocking tragedy that resonated with the people for many decades.

Angie was fully adjusted into city life during the 1940s and was well known for not only being the mother of several professional sons but also for her robust and assertive character. She was a friendly woman, but there was an autocratic air about her which commanded respect.

Religion played an important part in Angie's life and she attended Mass every morning. At the front of the Church were pews with plaques engraved with the names of particular members of the congregation who had paid to have seats reserved for their exclusive use. Angie objected to the practice. It was, in her opinion, a form of segregation that should not be tolerated in the House of God. She decided to make a stand by operating a 'one woman' campaign. This took the form of Angie purposefully planting herself in a reserved seat each day and stubbornly refusing to budge on request. After many weeks of unrelenting protest, Church Administrators caved in and the policy relating to hired pews was suspended. Angie felt gratified that her robust and unwavering action had achieved the desired outcome.

When her grand-daughters complained that they were being physically and verbally abused by a particular nun at the Convent, Angie presented herself at the school and confronted the accused with tongue-lashing words of reprehension, concluding that, even though her girls were black, the colour of the money being paid for their education was the same as the fees they received for every other student who attended the Convent.

No further abusive incidents were reported following the assertive action taken by Angie in her endeavour to protect her charges. On the contrary, the girls commented on how pleasant the nun had become in her interactions with them following their grandmother's unannounced visit to the Convent.

The Presentation College was the first Roman Catholic Secondary School for boys in Grenada. The school, which had been erected in St George's town, was opened in 1946. The maximum age for admission was 14. Angie was determined that her beloved 16-year-old grandson should not miss out on the opportunity of a secondary education, even though he was above the age limit for admission. She decided to act by putting forward sound and persuasive written reasons for consideration in making him an exception. College Administrators were swayed by Angie's compelling arguments and decided to waive the criteria in favour of her grandson. Angie, who desired the best educational opportunities for all her children, felt that she had won the 'star prize' and was deliriously happy.

The end of the Second World War in May 1945 was welcomed by the nation with immense joy and relief. News that the war had been won by the Allies quickly spread throughout the island and people spilled onto the streets in large numbers. There were firework displays and triumphant singing and dancing. It had been a jubilant and victorious moment in time.

Angie's youngest son, Thomas, who had been recruited by the British Merchant Navy, decided on taking the risk of absconding when his ship docked in the United States at the end of the war. Despite having no legal right of entry, Thomas was intent on finding a niche on the vast continent.

In the meantime, Angie was becoming increasingly concerned about the whereabouts of her youngest son. She prayed that he was safe and well and that he would one day resume contact with the family. But it was not to be. Angie would never again lay eyes on Thomas or have any form of contact with him during her remaining years. She would not know that Thomas had gained entry to Howard Medical School in Washington, DC, and had almost completed his studies in Paediatric Medicine when his illegal status was discovered by the Authorities. Thomas escaped to Chicago, changed his name and married an African-American.

Angie was overcome with grief when, in 1946, she attended the funeral of her beloved mother Dee Dee, accompanied by her sons and daughters. Dee Dee was remembered for being a compassionate, supportive and generous mother and grandmother. She was also a devoted wife who worked alongside her husband to ensure a future economic platform for their offspring. In her own right, Dee Dee was a comparatively sophisticated woman with unshakeable self-esteem and mental strength.

Angie was particularly distressed when, two years following the passing of her beloved mother, her favourite grandson left Grenada to join his mother and older sisters in the United States. But she was satisfied that she had always acted in his best interests and ensured that he received the very best educational opportunities available on the island at the time. Angie would no doubt have been delighted to learn that, after enlisting in the United States Army and serving in the Korean War, her adored 'Sonny' would be successful in his chosen career as a Professor of Dentistry.

After the departure of her grandson, Angie continued to care for the youngest grand-daughter, who had been deeply saddened to be separated from her older siblings.

It was a period when Eileen and Rosie were also residing at the family home. Rosie had returned after separating from her husband. Angie mourned the fact that the marriages of both Clarice and Rosie failed and was often being heard to say, "My girls are unlucky in love". Always philosophical, Angie believed that everything in life came at a cost and felt that her daughters' misfortune with men may have been the price she paid for producing so many successful sons.

The years of caring for young children had finally come to an end and Angie appeared mellowed. She became less critical and more praising. In particular, Eileen, whose love of glamour and fashion had been met with disapproval, suddenly found herself the subject of admiration. Angie commended the way her youngest daughter fixed her abundance of beautiful hair in the upsweep fashion of the day and praised her creative needlework and dressmaking skills with the words, "Eileen, you are an artist with a needle." These positive comments were totally uncharacteristic of Angie, but Eileen was delighted and cherished her mother's uplifting compliments for the rest of her life.

Despite twenty years of child-bearing, Angie sustained robust health and fitness and had been ill on only two occasions during her adult life. She suffered extreme exhaustion and was unwell for several weeks as a consequence of physically chastising O'Hanley shortly after giving birth. She was again laid low from the effects of a severe chill. Apart from painful knees, Angie was essentially well and felt that she would live to a ripe old age.

In June 1948, Angie, with her daughters and grand-daughter, moved into a new house purchased by Dr John as a special gift to his mother. The house was small and compact and, most importantly, located in close proximity to the Church which Angie attended on a daily basis. The house backed onto the island's main Courthouse and the family were intrigued by interesting or scandalous revelations that could be clearly heard during proceedings.

Two weeks had flown by and Angie had already happily settled in her perfect little house when the fateful day in July 1948 arrived. It began with worrying news from a messenger that Angie's favourite brother, Limmix, who lived with his family in the village of Dudmar, St David's, was seriously unwell. Angie rushed to her brother's side and wasted no time preparing the herbal mixture she believed would be 'good for him'. As anticipated, Limmix found the remedy soothing and was feeling 'a little better' by the time Angie was ready to begin her journey back home. She assured her brother that she would be back at his bedside the following day.

As Angie made her way to a junction to catch the bus back to town, she was suddenly overcome with dizziness and sought assistance from the people who lived nearby.

Supported by the concerned individuals, Angie was taken inside, helped onto a chair and offered a bottle of milk stout. It was a well-intended gesture by those who assumed that she simply lacked strength and would benefit from the energy drink. Angie was helped on to the bus when it arrived and delivered directly to her front door. Rosie and Eileen were alarmed to see the dramatic change in their mother, who was fine when she left for St David's just hours previously. They bravely concealed their sense of panic and assisted her into bed.

Dr John was called and he hurried to his mother's side. The symptoms indicated that she had suffered a stroke, but John was concerned to hear from Angie that she had been given a milk stout by well-meaning country folk. He was mindful that the beverage might not have been helpful to her condition. John arranged round-the-clock nursing care for his mother, but Angie's need for privacy and dignity prevailed and she would only allow daughters Rosie and Eileen to deliver her personal care.

Angie remained bedbound for one week and during that time the house was continuously filled with family members, friends and well-wishers. Despite being physically restricted by her illness, Angie was astute and observant and her spirit remained high. She cracked jokes and engaged in juicy gossip, but many a quiet moment was spent in silent prayer. Angie was able to derive a sense of peace from the surrounding natural environment. She was soothed by the cool breeze that rushed in from the opened window at night time and revitalised by the sunshine that shone through during the day. She assessed the greenery of the garden and predicted that the forthcoming crop would be bountiful.

There was general dismay when the message arrived that Limmix had lost his battle with illness, but every effort was made to shield Angie from the distressing news. Not surprisingly, everyone in the house was shocked when Angie suddenly announced that she knew Lemmix was 'dead'!

As Angie's condition deteriorated, relatives and friends gathered around her bed in prayer. A Priest was called and the Last Rites were administered. Lloyd, who had been practising on the island of Trinidad where he lived with his wife and family, returned home after receiving news of Angie's critical condition. He was shattered to see how desperately ill she was and immediately broke into uncontrollable sobs. As a boy, Lloyd always felt the need to protect his mother when William was away from home, by sharing her bed. He was now consumed with similar emotions, but despaired that he could do nothing to shield her from the grim outcome of this dreadful illness. He climbed into bed with his mother and held her close. Lloyd's warm body lying beside her was reassuringly comforting for Angie. He had been her protector as a boy and her very last words were spoken to him. She said, "Son, I knew you would come. Your mother is dying, you know." Lloyd shivered as a wave of ice-cold dread washed over him. He said nothing, but tightened his arms around his mother and prayed.

Angie had been in deep and tranquil sleep when Lloyd eased himself out of her bed for what was intended would be a short period of time before returning. He had no idea that she had been lulled into a final peaceful slumber by his tangible and comforting presence. A few short minutes after Lloyd had left Angie's side, the Duty Nurse was alerted by changes in her breathing and called for Rosie and Eileen. The sisters hurried to their mother's side and held her hand as she slipped away. They described her passing as being 'beautiful' and 'peaceful', similar to laboured breaths taken on a hill climb and the sigh of relief and subsequent calm on reaching the top. Angie passed away in July 1948, nine days after she had been struck down by a stroke.

The family were unable to make contact with O'Hanley, Tox or Thomas to inform them of the bereavement, as their whereabouts were unknown.

Lincoln had been in his internship as a newly qualified physician at a hospital in New York when he received news of his mother's illness. He was shaken by a further telegram informing him of her death. Lincoln immediately despatched a return telegram stating that he was on his way home and intended to be one of the pallbearers.

A full Requiem Mass was held for Angie at the Roman Catholic Cathedral in St George's town and the church was filled to capacity. The coffin was carried by sons Ivan, John, Lloyd, Daniel and Alban. Lincoln, who should also have been a pallbearer, had not arrived as expected.

The skies were grey with lingering dark clouds on the day of Angie's funeral. An aircraft circled noisily during the service. The congregation was oblivious to the fact that Lincoln was a passenger on the airplane and that it had been experiencing landing difficulties because of the adverse weather.

At the end of the Mass, the cortege, which included 10 buses and 50 cars packed with mourners, proceeded slowly to the Cemetery at Windsor Forest in the parish of St David's. On arrival, prayers for the soul of Angie were led by a Priest and hymns were bellowed amidst much weeping and wailing. Angie was finally laid to rest alongside her beloved husband William.

When Lincoln eventually appeared, Angie had already been buried. He was crestfallen to have missed his mother's funeral and even though it was due to circumstances that were out of his control, Lincoln's grief was intensified by feelings of guilt and regret.

POSTSCRIPT

Lincoln did not return to New York. He remained on the island, where he practised as a doctor for many years. He also held the position of Head Pharmacist in the pharmacy he owned in St George's town. Various business initiatives followed and included owning, training and racing horses. Lincoln, who was once deemed an academic failure, emerged as the most enterprising and ambitiously driven of the brothers. Lincoln never remarried, but maintained his fascination for women and pursued them throughout his life.

After many years abroad, O'Hanley and Tox returned to the homeland. They were shocked and devastated on hearing of their mother's passing and both found solace in alcohol. The brothers never married, but O'Hanley had fathered a son during his time in Columbia. Tox had no children.

Lloyd returned permanently to the homeland with his family and operated a busy dental practice in St George's town.

Alban and Daniel set up separate law and optical practices respectively, also in the town of St George's. The brothers would later follow different paths.

John maintained a successful medical service in various parishes across Grenada and also on the sister island of Carriacou.

Although he was known to be resident in the United States, Thomas remained elusive.

Clarice continued to live and work in New York.

Several years following Angie's demise, Rosie and Eileen immigrated to the United Kingdom and started a new life in London.

Ivan maintained a simple country lifestyle.

EPILOGUE

Angie had been last in a line of three generations of first daughters who hailed from a chauvinistic community in which women were expected to know their place and were generally undervalued and disrespected.

Hope, Dee Dee and Angie were strong-minded women of substance equipped with inherent self-esteem. The women were resolute in their principles but, with different approaches, succeeded in realising their individual personal objectives.

Hope endeavoured to free herself from a life of toil, but more importantly needed to gain control of her life. In her quest to realise her dream of independence and a better quality of life, Hope made the ultimate sacrifice by deserting her family. It was at the time an unimaginably daring undertaking and no other woman in her community had previously been known to take such a bold step.

The eldest abandoned daughter, Dee Dee, inherited her mother's innate indelible spirit and strength of character, which she used diplomatically but effectively. These traits were passed on to Angie, whose methods were transparently robust and assertive.

The educational foundation that had been put into place by an ambitious and inspirational father was no doubt the springboard for the academic successes of the sons of Angie and William Radix. But it was also the confidence and single mindedness, inherited from the maternal side of the family, that propelled the brothers into fulfilling ambitions considered unattainable by people of their kind and from their community of the period.

It was unusual that six of nine brothers from a largely disadvantaged community would be successful in a professional capacity. The men were celebrated for their remarkable and inspiring accomplishments during an era when home-grown professional practitioners were rare. They were respected for their empathetic and compassionate manner that was primarily motivated by a strong sense of vocation.

Hope could not have imagined that the grandchildren of the eldest daughter that was abandoned on a sleepy, humble, but hard-working country community would progress to the top of the hill on the very island that was deemed to offer very few opportunities or openings into a successful life.

Lightning Source UK Ltd.
Milton Keynes UK
UKOW04f0107130514

231551UK00001B/4/P